Peace

for the

Troubled Heart

Richard Caldwell

Published by:
Kress Biblical Resources
www.kressbiblical.com

ISBN: 978-1-934952-65-8

Contents

Psalm 4
Peace in Turbulent Times
Psalm 4

To the choirmaster: with stringed

instruments. A Psalm of David.

[1] Answer me when I call, O God of my righteousness!
You have given me relief when I was in distress.
Be gracious to me and hear my prayer!
[2] O men, how long shall my honor be turned into shame?
How long will you love vain words and seek after lies?
Selah
[3] But know that the LORD has set apart the godly for himself;
the LORD hears when I call to him.

[4] Be angry, and do not sin;
ponder in your own hearts on your beds, and be silent.
Selah
[5] Offer right sacrifices,
and put your trust in the LORD.

[6] There are many who say, "Who will show us some good?
Lift up the light of your face upon us, O LORD!"
[7] You have put more joy in my heart
than they have when their grain and wine abound.

[8] In peace I will both lie down and sleep;
for you alone, O LORD, make me dwell in safety.

Psalm 4 has been called an evening Psalm. It's not hard to understand why. In the 8th verse, as David is ending the Psalm, he says *In peace I will both lie down and sleep....* We need a Psalm like this. We need an evening Psalm, because, as you well know, it's often in the darkness of the day that we experience the darkness in our soul, the darkness of the heart.

Have you ever known that experience, where in the middle of the night, the things that bothered you during the day seem to grow larger? The anxieties increase. The worries seem to loom so large that sometimes you have trouble sleeping. Maybe what is going on in your heart has to do with some physical ailment. Maybe you're thinking about your health, and what the future will hold for you. Maybe it has to do with finances. Maybe you are looking for work, and not able to find it. Maybe at night you are lying in your bed and wondering when the job is going to come, and how you'll survive until the job comes.

Sometimes, what is troubling us has to do with a relationship. Maybe someone has hurt you. Maybe you find yourself estranged from someone you love. Or maybe it has to do with a loved one who has gone astray, and you're concerned about their spiritual condition. During the day you've made it okay, but at night it seems to grow larger in your mind and in your heart. Or, maybe it's not a relational problem. Maybe you just feel lonely. You feel alone in the middle of the night. What do you do with that?

One commentator wrote, "The approach of night with its temptation to brood on past wrongs and present perils only challenges David to make his faith explicit, and to urge it on others as a committal of one's cause and one's self to a faithful Creator."[1]

That's what we do with what we wrestle with in the night. And we know that many times what we're wrestling with is not fictitious. It's real. There are real dangers, real threats. What do you do with those things?

The answer is this: you must meditate on God's fatherly love for you. In our church, we sometimes sing about the fact that our Father loves us, that we are His children.[2] We need to meditate on that. We need to meditate on God's faithfulness to His people. We need to reflect on how faithful God has been to us throughout our lives, how we can see His faithful love for us throughout our spiritual journey, and then understand that God doesn't change, and His love for us doesn't change.

We can expect in the future more of what we have seen of God's faithfulness in our past. That's why we must take those worries, those anxieties, those things that we know threaten us, those real dangers, and put those things where they really are anyway, into the hands of God. And we must trust Him. It's only in that place of sincere trust that we can be at peace and lie down and sleep. That's what David tells us about here.

He is under some sort of major stress. The exact historical circumstances that gave rise to this Psalm are unclear. Some have seen in this Psalm perhaps what David

---

[1] Derek Kidner, *Psalms 1-72: An Introduction and Commentary*, vol. 15, Tyndale Old Testament Commentaries (Downers Grove, IL: InterVarsity Press, 1973), 72.
[2] "We Sing as One" by Young Oceans.
https://www.youtube.com/watch?v=RQ49jaDYess

experienced when he was running from Saul. They look at the statements there where it says, *How long...how long...how long?* and they think, "He endured a long time of suffering at the hands of Saul. Maybe that's what this has to do with."

I personally lean in the direction that this Psalm has a connection with the previous Psalm, Psalm 3. Psalm 3 has been referred to as a morning hymn because of verse 5, *I lay down and slept; I woke again, for the Lord sustained me.* In Psalm 4, you go to sleep trusting God. In Psalm 3, you wake up and He has sustained you. The superscription to the 3rd Psalm tells us that that it's a Psalm of David when he fled from Absalom, his son.

These two Psalms are very much alike, both in their structure and in their subject matter. David is in distress, under attack. His heart is troubled. And yet, he is witnessing God's faithful hand of protection upon his life. And so, I think, if we're looking for a historical circumstance that might have given rise to this Psalm, it may have been when he was experiencing trouble at the hands of Absalom.

It really doesn't matter. Regardless of the historical circumstances, this Psalm is meant to serve the people of God in their times of trouble. The very fact that it is a part of the public worship of the people of God means this does not just apply to David. This applies to you and to me. These things are true when we are hurting. They are true when we are tempted to be afraid. These things are true when we find ourselves under attack, when we feel like we are surrounded by enemies. It doesn't matter what's looming large in the night watches, what is troubling your heart, what is keeping you awake—these things are true. You can rest in them. You can count on them.

This psalm celebrates the covenant faithfulness of God. David is not just a man of God. He's God's anointed king, the King of Israel. And so, it's not just David's person that God is defending in this Psalm. The Lord is defending David's position in the life of the nation of Israel. And in that way, God is defending the nation. This is an example of God's faithfulness to all of His people, including His servant David.

Psalm 4 is really a three-way conversation. David is talking to the Lord. David is talking to men. David is talking to himself. He's talking to the Lord, and in the context of his conversation with God, he is speaking in his heart concerning his enemies, and he is speaking in his heart concerning his own life.

I'm sure you recognize this is what we do when we're in the midst of trouble and turmoil. We talk to God. And as we commune with the Lord, we are also in our hearts thinking about those who are troubling us, if it's a relational issue, and we also think about our lives. What are we going to do? Where are we going to go? What does this mean for me, or for my family? So, if you've ever felt the mental distress of conflict, you can easily identify with what David writes here. And if you have not yet known that kind of mental distress, just wait. Eventually, you will, so keep your Bible marked at Psalm 4.

We can organize this Psalm into three parts, easy to follow:

- Speaking to God, verse 1

- Speaking to men, verses 2-5

- Speaking to God (again), verses 6-8

The conversation begins with God. The conversation ends with God. And in the middle, he considers his enemies.

Speaking to God, :1

Psalm 4:1 *Answer me when I call, O God of my righteousness! You have given me relief when I was in distress. Be gracious to me and hear my prayer!*

Where do you turn in the dark times? You turn to God. Twice in verse 1, David cries out for God to hear him. John Calvin wrote, "As he asks twice to be heard, in this there is expressed to us both the vehemence of his grief, and the earnest of his prayers."[3] Why does he say twice, "Lord, hear me"? Well, because he feels this, and he also knows his desperate need for God. He is under the weight of what he's going to describe. He feels it. He's under the weight of it. The vehemence of his grief, but also it speaks of the earnestness of his prayers. He needs the Lord's help.

As we can see in other Psalms, as he cries out for this, he doesn't come to the Lord on the basis of his own merit. Notice what he says in verse 1. *Be gracious to me....* In other words, "Lord, I'm approaching You on the ground of mercy, in the light of Your mercy and Your grace." He doesn't imagine that he deserves anything, but he is confident of how his Defender views him, how God has related Himself to David. So, he comes in a dependent fashion, not a presumptuous fashion.

But if he's not coming based upon his own merit, what does he mean when he says, *O God of my righteousness!* ?

---

[3] John Calvin and James Anderson (translator), *Commentary on the Book of Psalms*, vol. 1 (Bellingham, WA: Logos Bible Software, 2010), 39.

He means simply that God is the Defender of his cause, and that his cause is right. God is the vindicator of His servant, of His people. It's not a statement about David's view of his own merit, but rather his view of God's faithfulness to His people, and to what is right, the kind of cause that, in a clear conscience, he knows he stands in.

And notice that David exhibits faith in future grace.[4] He has known God's grace in the past, and now approaches God in view of what God has done in the past as he looks to the future. He knows God's past grace is a demonstration of who God will be to him in the future. Where do we see that? In verse 1 he says, *You have given me relief....* That's a perfect tense verb. This is something that has been accomplished in the past. *You have given me relief when I was in distress.* In the word *distress* is the idea of narrowness, constriction. David has known what it is to be in tight spots and see God set him out into the open. He has known the delivering, preserving, powerful hand of God on his behalf, so as he thinks about what he's presently facing, he asks for this again.

May I encourage you to do something? When your heart is afraid in the night watches, take a moment as you cry out to God to remember that He has been faithful to you already, so He will be faithful to you here, and He will be faithful to you in the future. That's who He is.

Speaking to Men, :2-5

This perspective of God now transforms his view of his enemies. Verses 2-5 have been viewed in three different ways. Some people see verses 2-5 all referring to the people

---

[4] For more about "Future Grace," see John Piper's book by that title.

of God, to godly people. Maybe they're struggling, maybe they're in doubt, but each of these verses has something to say to the people of God. Derek Kidner is an example of someone who takes this view.

The *ESV Study Bible* takes verses 2 and 3 as referring to David's enemies, then verses 4 and 5, as words to the godly.

I take the view, agreeing with Calvin, MacArthur and others, that David is speaking to his enemies throughout verses 2-5. In verse 2, he begins, *O men*, literally, *O sons of men, how long shall my honor be turned into shame? How long will you love vain words and seek after lies?* These are clearly David's enemies, and there is no indication that he changes his audience as he speaks here. These verses all seem to refer to David's enemies, and this demonstrates what trust in God will do, in terms of transforming your view of what threatens you. In David's case, he's being threatened by people, and he goes from verse 1 in which he expresses trust in the Lord to these statements in which he is standing in amazement that his enemies would take such a posture against him.

As we'll see in a moment, he's saying in effect, "If you only knew how God has related Himself to me, and to all of His people, you would not be doing what you're doing." He warns his enemies in verses 2-5. It's an amazing thing to witness.

David's awareness

Now, before we see what he says to them, notice what he's aware of in verses 2-5. What are they doing, these enemies of his? They are **dishonoring** him.

Psalm 4:2a *O [sons of] men, how long shall my honor be turned into shame?*

They are treating him in a way that does not recognize the fact that he is the Lord's anointed king. They seek to humiliate him, disregarding his honor and treating him shamefully instead.

They also dishonor him by **defaming** him.

Psalm 4:2b *How long will you love vain words and seek after lies? Selah*

This could speak either of what they're practicing or what they're searching for. They would love vain words and they would seek after lies in the sense that they practice this. This is what they run after, what they pursue. It's how they live. This is what they're practicing toward David. Or, it could mean they are enemies searching for these empty words and these lies in order to defame him. "Let me find words that would ruin David's reputation."

Now, if the historical situation really is connected with Psalm 3, it's not hard to envision what this kind of behavior looks like. Even if this is not connected to Psalm 3, the history of Absalom, David's son who tried to be king, is an illustration of what this kind of behavior looks like.

2 Samuel 15:1 *After this Absalom got himself a chariot and horses, and fifty men to run before him.* [2] *And Absalom used to rise early and stand beside the way of the gate. And when any man had a dispute to come before the king for judgment, Absalom would call to him and say, "From what city are you?" And when he said, "Your servant is of such and such a tribe in Israel,"* [3] *Absalom would say to him, "See, your claims are good and right, but there is no*

*man designated by the king to hear you." * ⁴ Then Absalom
would say, "Oh that I were judge in the land! Then every
man with a dispute or cause might come to me, and I
would give him justice.' ⁵ And whenever a man came near
to pay homage to him, he would put out his hand and take
hold of him and kiss him. ⁶ Thus Absalom did to all of
Israel who came to the king for judgment. So Absalom
stole the hearts of the men of Israel.*

This is a man who is shaming his father, lying about his
father and undermining him while flattering people. Verse
5 is especially striking. They would come to pay him
homage, but he would treat them as friends. "I'm one with
you." And he stole the hearts of the men of Israel.

My friend, this is not just Absalom. Oh, what a bright
unmistakable example of this kind of behavior, but this is
just sinful humanity. And long before these attitudes get
expressed with the mouth, they begin to exist in the heart.
"If that were me, things would be different," so that in their
own mind, they become the protector of the people. But in
truth, they're just exalting themselves.

May I warn you about this, and warn myself also? We
must be careful to recognize that the Lord takes care of His
people, and that God has assigned to us different roles with
different responsibilities. We can trust the Lord to work
through those whom He places in positions to shepherd
people. There are legitimate ways to defend people. There
are people who need to be defended. But history is full of
people who presented themselves as a shepherd, when in
reality they were a wolf. And they play on the emotions of
people to assume the role that exalts them.

Let me give you some examples. I've seen this happen
with marriages. During my decades of pastoral ministry.

I've seen men who want to be the defender for someone else's wife. Here's how it happens. First, you begin to think in your mind, "He doesn't treat her the right way." And then maybe you even see him mistreat her in some way. Before long, you put yourself into the place of the defender of someone else's wife. I cannot tell you how many times adultery has had its door opened with that kind of thinking.[5]

I've seen this happen with parenting. "Oh, I feel so sorry for those children," and in your mind you begin to think, "If I were his parent...," "If I were her parent...." I have to confess that as a grandfather, I sometimes think that way, even though my grandchildren have great parents. I have to remind myself that God gave my grandchildren to their own parents. Would I do it different sometimes? Of course. They would have done it different than me sometimes. The point is, God assigned those children to them. And unless it's a sin issue, I need to trust the Lord to work in that situation.

The point is that we begin to put ourselves in the wrong mindset. You see this happening with people working in an organization. They begin to criticize their superior. They begin to talk to their fellow workers. "Oh, if I were in charge, this is what it would be like." I've seen it happen with wicked people in the church.

Something like this is going on with David. People are shaming him and slandering him. So, what does he do? How

---

[5] There are women who need to be defended from an abusive husband, but if you don't have equal love and concern for both the husband and the wife, constantly guarding against wanting to be the hero, realizing that it's not your job to meet the woman's emotional needs, you're on highly dangerous ground.

do you respond to such attacks if you're the target of those attacks, or even the target of just the attitude?

David's appeal

We can learn from what David does. In verses 3-5, we find six imperatives—six commands—in which I believe he appeals to the wicked people. He both stands in amazement at the stance they have taken, and warns them about the outcomes of such attitudes and actions.

Psalm 4:3 *But know that the LORD has set apart*
the godly for himself;
the LORD hears when I call to him.
⁴ Be angry, and do not sin;
ponder in your own hearts on your beds,
and be silent. Selah
⁵ Offer right sacrifices,
and put your trust in the LORD.

Something you must know. :3

The first of the six imperatives, he says, is something they must know: *But know that the Lord has set apart the godly for himself; the Lord hears when I call to him.* In essence, "You who love lies, you who seek after vain words, or love vain words, seek after lies, you need to know that this isn't just true with me." I love the fact that he doesn't just say God has done this with him. He says God has done this for the godly. God has set apart His people, the godly, for Himself. which is to say, He has a special relationship with His people. He loves His people and is faithful to them. He defends them. David wants the evil people to know that when David calls to the Lord, the Lord hears him. Isn't it wonderful that David can see that? As a child of God, can you see that? If you're being mistreated, if you're being persecuted, if you're in the darkness of the night, and things are looming large in your mind, and you're afraid of people, do you stop and remind yourself that the Lord has set apart the godly for Himself? He is not ignoring you. He has a special relationship with you. And when you call, He hears you.

Something you must fear. :4a

In verse 4, David says, *Be angry, and do not sin.* The second imperative is something these enemies must fear.

People have taken this in two ways, because the Hebrew word translated *be angry* (רִגְזוּ rig·zū) could also be translated *tremble.* If it refers to anger, and if David is addressing this to his enemies, he is saying, "You need to control your anger; to put a harness on it. If you're going to smolder on the inside, you need to keep it on the inside." In fact, he will say later in the verse: *ponder in your own hearts on your beds, and be silent.* So, taking it this way, the idea is that they're angry, but instead of giving expression to it as they have been doing, with lies and vain words, they need to be careful not to sin. "You need to be afraid of sinning."

Perhaps *tremble* is the better way to understand this. So, the idea is "You need to be trembling, fearful over what you're doing. You need to tremble at your behavior and your words and your attitudes." Either way, he says, *Do not sin.*

Something you must consider. :4b

The third imperative is to *ponder in your own hearts on your beds.*

The word *ponder* means to meditate or to speak to yourselves. He's saying, "You need to do this *in your own hearts, on your beds*. They need to stop and think about what it is they're engaging in.

Something you must do. :4c

Then the fourth imperative, something they must do. He says, *be silent*—be quiet. David is saying, "Stop it. Think about it and stop it. These vain words, these lies—think about it, and stop it. Be afraid of what you're doing and think about it, and stop it. Be quiet."

There's another possibility, seen in the *NET Bible*. There's the possibility that this word translated "to be quiet" can mean to wail. And if that were to be the case—and I don't believe it is—but if that were to be the case, then the idea would still be the same thing. He's calling for repentance. "Stop doing what you're doing."

Something you must begin. :5a

He says, *Offer right sacrifices*— "Turn from an empty appearance of worship that is really offensive to God. Because of your spiritual condition, because of what you're engaging in, your worship is offensive to God. You need to offer right sacrifices."

As you know from elsewhere in the Old Testament, right sacrifices are not just sacrifices offered externally, but sacrifices offered with a genuine heart, with a broken, contrite spirit. He's calling for repentance.

Did you know that when Absalom was conspiring against his father, he was offering sacrifices?

2 Samuel 15:12 *And while Absalom was offering the sacrifices, he sent for Ahithophel the Gilonite, David's counselor, from his city Giloh. And the conspiracy grew strong, and the people with Absalom kept increasing.*

He was lying about his father, undermining his father, but all the while playing the part of the religious man, offering sacrifices while sending for his father's key counselor. The world is full of feigned worship. And you mark this: Wicked people are often very religious people. What do you desire for them? You want them to repent. What you want them to join in true worship. On a personal level, we don't long for their destruction, though we understand the justice of it if God were to do it. We long for their repentance. We long for their salvation.

Is there someone who has been attacking you? Is there someone who has set themselves in opposition to you? And I wonder, have you been longing for their personal destruction, or have you been longing for their repentance, and praying for their salvation? May God's love shine through you towards such a person, and may your trust in your God shine forth through your life so that they understand that you're not upset by them. You're at rest in the Lord. You long for their repentance.

Repent, so that your sacrifices—your worship—will be *right sacrifices*.

Someone to whom you must yield. :5b

He says at the end of verse 5, *and put your trust in the* LORD. True worship is the expression of humble trust. There is no true worship apart from humble trust. And so, he's calling upon his enemies to humbly bow the knee to God.

Do you know why wicked people do the things like Absalom did? It's because they're not true worshippers. They don't love God; therefore, they don't love God's people; therefore, they don't love you. And so, they begin to seek for themselves what they believe will satisfy their hearts instead of turning to God for the satisfaction of their hearts. Instead of entrusting themselves to God and longing in their hearts for His exaltation, they exalt themselves, thinking that it will bring satisfaction. That's what leads people to do the kind of thing that Absalom did. That, or continuing bitterness and hatred in the heart because of not forgiving someone. If we do that, we're not loving God, and we're not worshipping the Lord.

> The ungodly may indeed flatter and delude themselves, but when they are brought in good earnest to the trial [that is, when they stand before the Lord], it will always be clear that the reason why they are deceived is because from the beginning they were determined to deal deceitfully. For no matter what devices they use to assault us, if we have the testimony of a good conscience, God will remain on our side, and they shall not prevail against Him. They may greatly excel in ingenuity and possess much power of hurting us, and have their plans and subsidiary aide completely ready, and be very shrewd in discernment, yet whatever they may invent, it will be only lying and vanity.
> –John Calvin [6]

I love the way he set forth that case, because these are the things that loom before our minds in the middle of the night. "God, they are smart, and they have power, and they have plans, and they have people to help them, and they're

---

[6] John Calvin and James Anderson (translator), *Commentary on the Book of Psalms*, vol. 1 (Bellingham, WA: Logos Bible Software, 2010), 41-42; translation modernized for this book

shrewd." Calvin is saying, "But don't you recognize who they're forming their plans against? When they form their plans against the child of God, the godly person, they're forming their plans against the Lord. And those things will not prevail."

So, David speaks to God. And after speaking to God, you can see a transformed perspective of the people who threaten him. He warns them. He's not in danger. They're in danger. Did you get that? He's not in danger. They're in danger. What an amazing perspective of such a threat.

Speaking to God Again, :6-8

And so, where does this evening Psalm end? David talks to the Lord once more.

Psalm 4:6 *There are many who say,*
"Who will show us some good?
Lift up the light of your face upon us, O LORD!"
⁷ You have put more joy in my heart than they have
when their grain and wine abound.
⁸ In peace I will both lie down and sleep;
for you alone, O Lord, make me dwell in safety.

This is how we must process our problems and our fears. This is how we must process even those things that discourage us when we witness what we're seeing in the world at large. Maybe you're like me. Maybe your heart sinks a bit when you hear some of the news of your nation and the broader world. You look at your world and say, "This is a dark place." Here is how to process it: You process it sandwiched between conversation with God and conversation with God. That is, you must see these things in the context of our fellowship with God, and understand the greatness of the God with whom we have this

20

fellowship. He is on His throne, and, therefore, His people are really safe.

And so, like David, we process these troubles and these threats by confessing truth about the God of Israel, his God and our God.

David confesses three things.

We have a single source of hope. :6

In verse 6, David says, *There are many who say, "Who will show us some good?"* He is acknowledging that there are people in the nation of Israel who, due to whatever circumstances he is facing, are discouraged and despondent. They are wondering out loud, "Where is this all headed? Where are we going to find hope? Where is there some good?"

And what does he confess? *Lift up the light of your face upon us, O LORD!* That is, "We're looking to You for blessing. You're our hope." David is the king, and yet he writes this in a way that makes plain he's not the hope. People are asking, "Where is the good going to come from?" He doesn't say, "It will come from me, the king." He says, "Lord, I'm looking to You. Would You lift up Your face upon us? Would You shine Your face upon us? We look to You, Lord, for good things." Who will show us some good? God will show us good. We look to Him.

When you think about hope, do you have a single source? A I was preparing this study of Psalm 4, a good man in government died suddenly. My hope is not tied to such a man, though I appreciate the way he served our country. He was not my hope. We have one source of hope. Our hope is the living God.

We have a superior source of joy. :7

Verse 7: *You have put more joy in my heart than they have when their grain and wine abound.* He's saying, "Take note of what makes worldlings happy. Notice the joy of lost people—what they rejoice over, what they throw a party over, what makes their day."

We all used to be like that. I'm so thankful when the Lord saves children, early in life. It's a blessing. But there's also blessing to getting saved later in life, because you can remember a life where your joys were misplaced. I can remember the days when I knew a joy outside of God. I can identify with what David confesses here. That is, God has filled my heart with joys I never knew in my lost condition. As a believer, you see people without the Lord who are celebrating because of their favorable circumstances, and you think as David does in verse 7, "Lord, You—<u>You</u> have put more joy into my heart than they have on their very best day. "Lord, You've given me joy."

So, my source of hope is the Lord, and my source of joy is the Lord. You can know that joy no matter what's going on in the world, no matter what's going on in your life, no matter what the threat is. When you really have this perspective of God, your dark moment of the night can turn into a hallelujah party. It can turn into a celebration of God's faithfulness if you just begin to think rightly about whatever it is that has you afraid.

David can say these things because of what he says in verse 8.

We have a certain source of safety. :8

In verse 8, David says, *In peace I will both lie down and sleep.* I like that. He doesn't say, "I'm going to lie down with one eye open. I have all these people after me, so when I lie down, I'll keep an eye open to make sure I'm okay." He says, "I'm going to *both lie down and sleep.* Why? Because *You alone, Yahweh, make me dwell in safety.*"

There's only one reason any of us is ever safe—the living God who sits in the heavens and does as He pleases, the sovereign God who guarantees your life until He's finished with you. There's a sense in which you are indestructible until His purpose for you is done on this side of your everlasting existence with Him in the age that's coming. So that you are never in a place where you're not safe—never.

What is the explanation for the safety of a human being? David confesses, "My safety is You, God. You make me safe." Work that out. Think about that. Your money doesn't make you safe. All these relationship ties you try to form with people who will stand up for you and defend you, that doesn't make you safe. Your own reasoning, staying up late at night thinking about all the angles, and who might be coming at you—that doesn't make you safe.

Do you want to know how to lie down and sleep? Realize that the Lord makes you safe.

Psalm 127:1 *A song of ascents. Of Solomon. Unless the LORD builds the house, those who build it labor in vain. Unless the Lord watches over the city, the watchman stays awake in vain.*

Do you sit on the wall as a watchman? You're staying awake? Oh, God works through means. The watchmen ought to be there. But unless the Lord is defending that city, you can flood the walls with watchmen, and it's won't be safe.

David says, *In peace I will both lie down and sleep; for you alone, O LORD, make me dwell in safety.* Thank God that in the night watches we don't have to give our minds to lies. We can give our mind to truth, and we can lie down, and we can go to sleep.

Psalm 39
The Wise Response to a Troubled Heart

Psalm 39

To the choirmaster: to Jeduthun. A Psalm of David.

[1] I said, "I will guard my ways,
    that I may not sin with my tongue;
I will guard my mouth with a muzzle,
    so long as the wicked are in my presence."
[2] I was mute and silent;
    I held my peace to no avail,
and my distress grew worse.
    [3] My heart became hot within me.
As I mused, the fire burned;
    then I spoke with my tongue:

[4] "O LORD, make me know my end
    and what is the measure of my days;
    let me know how fleeting I am!
[5] Behold, you have made my days a few handbreadths,
    and my lifetime is as nothing before you.
Surely all mankind stands as a mere breath! Selah
    [6] Surely a man goes about as a shadow!
Surely for nothing [a] they are in turmoil;
    man heaps up wealth and does not know who will
gather!

[7] "And now, O LORD, for what do I wait?
    My hope is in you.
[8] Deliver me from all my transgressions.
    Do not make me the scorn of the fool!
[9] I am mute; I do not open my mouth,
    for it is you who have done it.
[10] Remove your stroke from me;

I am spent by the hostility of your hand.
11 When you discipline a man
    with rebukes for sin,
you consume like a moth what is dear to him;
    surely all mankind is a mere breath! Selah

12 "Hear my prayer, O LORD,
    and give ear to my cry;
hold not your peace at my tears!
For I am a sojourner with you,
    a guest, like all my fathers.
13 Look away from me, that I may smile again,
    before I depart and am no more!"

a **6** Hebrew *Surely as a breath*

INTRODUCTION

Our world is full of pleasures. Despite the curses that were given after the fall, this life is full of all kinds of pleasure. We know pleasure in the realm of the senses: sight, sound, touch, taste, and smell. There are lots of things to enjoy. For example, just think about your favorite meal, and how pleasing it is to you. We know pleasure in the realm of thought and in the realm of expression: art, music, and literature. There are joys in the realm of relationships. Especially as believers, if we have a Christian marriage, what a joy that is to us. We have joy in our children, who are gifts from the Lord, and pleasures involved in raising them. There are pleasures in accomplishments. When we achieve, accomplish or finish something, even something as small as a garden or a woodcraft project, or something else, we have joy and pleasure in that.

But this world is under a curse, and pleasures that are known in it are usually fleeting. They do not ultimately satisfy. It's like living in a world full of echoes. These temporal pleasures are reminders of a time that has been lost. The pleasures we know <u>today</u> speak of a time in the <u>yesterday</u>, a time before sin, a time that we've never known. There was a much better time, a time before the fall and before there was separation from God.

In fact, the pleasures known by the lost man are the emptiest kind of pleasures. They are merely sensual. These pleasures are the best you can get when you are a blind, dead, slave to Satan, who is a cruel master. They are the best you can get when you have no true understanding of the Creator's purpose for a human life, and therefore no true sense of your own purpose.

Do you realize, when you are driving on a road crowded with cars, how many of those people have no true understanding of the Creator's purpose for mankind, and no true understanding of their own purpose on this planet? The result is that all those pleasures that men know, prove to be phantoms. They don't last. They leave people empty. The pleasures run away from them due to the robbing, ruinous nature of sin.

Things in this world that begin by being beautiful, often end up ugly. Do you have a friendship, for example, that has been ruined by sin? Do you remember the days that now seem to be almost like a dream? You wish you could go back to those times when there was joy, peace, unity, and fellowship, but the friendship has been ruined by sin, and it's gone.

The world is full of things like that, pleasures that run away from us because of the reality of aging and the disappearance of youth. Have you experienced this? It doesn't seem so long ago that you were young, but now you're not able to do the activities you once enjoyed.

Some pleasures run away from us because of the presence of sickness and human frailty. We encounter people every day who deal with the daily pains associated with the frailty of our humanness. Other pleasures run away from us because of the loss that we know through death. As we get older, more and more of our family pass away. Friends pass away. Acquaintances pass away, and our circle of relationships becomes smaller. We confront the reality of mortality.

On the brighter side, it's true that we as believers know pleasures that the world doesn't have access to. Those have come from the hand of God. But even as believers, we come face-to-face with the brutal realities of this world. Creation is described metaphorically as groaning for redemption, waiting for the revelation of the sons of God, because there will be the revelation of the Son of God. There will be new heavens, a new earth, and freedom from the bondage of the curse. If the world metaphorically groans for redemption, and the Bible says we do as well, then that means even believers know what it is to live in a very difficult place.

Romans 8:18 *For I consider that the sufferings of this present time are not worth comparing with the glory that is to be revealed to us. * *[19] For the creation waits with eager longing for the revealing of the sons of God. * *[20] For the creation was subjected to futility, not willingly, but because of him who subjected it, in hope * *[21] that the creation itself will be set free from its bondage to corruption and obtain the freedom of the glory of the children of God. * *[22] For we know that the whole creation has been groaning together in the pains of childbirth until now. * *[23] And not only the creation, but we ourselves, who have the firstfruits of the Spirit, groan inwardly as we wait eagerly for adoption as sons, the redemption of our bodies.*

When we were young, we didn't think much about things like the brevity and the difficulties of life. In those days, life seemed to be all sunshine, and not many clouds. But as we have become older, and if our wisdom has increased, the more we have seen that much of life in this present world really is vanity. Even today, there are many people who don't like to think about these sorts of things, saying, "Just keep moving. Stay busy. Stay entertained. Get up in the morning. Keep yourself busy. Lie down at night. Then repeat. Don't think too much about where it's all headed, what it all means. Just keep existing."

Do you realize the gift you have when you're in a relationship with God, and learn of the brevity and difficulty of life, that you're able to reflect on eternity? But when you reflect on these things apart from a relationship with God, you become depressed and cynical. If you're learning these lessons in a relationship with God, the result is not despair, but faith, love, and hope for eternal life. It leads to wisdom, which leads to the kind of life that really counts. It's a gift to be able to understand the difference between what is temporal and what is eternal. It's a gift when God teaches you about the brevity and difficulty of life, about the eternity that is coming. It's foolishness to treat temporal things as if they are eternal.

Overview

In Psalm 39, we find David contemplating the brevity and difficulty of life and, therefore, thinking about the true meaning of life. He has a problem that troubles him greatly, but doesn't specify what it is. We can benefit from his vagueness, because that allows us to put our own situation into it, wherever it is that we're being made conscious of life's brevity and difficulty.

Although we don't know what David's particular problem was, we do know is that this is an individual lament. This is one man's sorrows, one man's troubling questions. But wisdom never stops at its own condition. Wisdom then takes the individual lesson and uses it to reflect on the larger questions of life. And that's what David does here. He considers what's happening in his own life and reflects on life as a whole, and about mankind in general. His approach is wise, and we do well to listen to him as in this psalm the Holy Spirit through David gives us the Word of God. It leads us to reflect on the brevity of life, the difficulty of life, and the meaning of life.

Psalm 39 has been <u>organized</u> by commentators in a number of different ways. An easy way to consider it effectively is by dividing it into two parts. In verses 1-6, we see **a commitment worked out**. In view of his perplexity, in view of his troubled heart, David makes a commitment he then works out. Then in verse 7, there is **his confession worked out**. This the high point of the Psalm, and in some ways, you might even say a turning point. So, you have a commitment worked out, verses 1-6, and a confession worked out, verses 7-13.

As we walk through this Psalm, notice that there's a pattern. David will request something, and then reflect on what he requests. There's a request and then a reflection, a request, then a reflection, a request, then a reflection.

David's Commitment

First, notice the commitment David makes in view of his troubled heart. **<u>Something is happening inside of him, but he's made a commitment.</u>**

Verse 1: *I said, "I will guard my ways, that I may not sin with my tongue; I will guard my mouth with a muzzle, so long as the wicked are in my presence." I was mute and silent; I held my peace to no avail, and my distress grew worse. My heart became hot within me. As I mused, the fire burned; then I spoke with my tongue....*

He begins this Psalm with something very valuable because it sets the tone for the entire Psalm. He's going to tell us about his frustrations, but before revealing them, he wants us to know that they do not speak of irreverence or disloyalty. David reverences God, even while he's dealing with trouble in his heart. We know this, because he tells us that he made a <u>commitment so as not to sin.</u> He's aware of the possibility of sin, but he doesn't want to sin. So even as he's battling this problem within himself, he's doing it in the context of reverence for God and not in sinful anger. He remains loyal to the Lord, because he doesn't want to say anything that would dishonor God in the presence of wicked people, verse 1: *I will guard my mouth with a muzzle, so long as the wicked are in my presence.* This is a man who fears God. He's loyal to the Lord and jealous for His glory.

David's example is important for us to think about because we also deal with frustrations, even while we fear the Lord, and even while we are jealous for the glory of God. We can be honest and be transparent about the fact that there are things that trouble us. We could say it this way: there are things that we wish were different. We don't say it irreverently nor disloyally. It's just true.

His commitment reflects **wisdom**. <u>David is wise to know his propensity for sin.</u> Why does he say he's going to put a guard on his ways by muzzling his speech? Because he knows he is capable of sinning, especially in the midst of this frustration. He doesn't want to sin, so he's committed to disciplining himself in his speech, so as not to sin. That's a godly man. "I don't want to dishonor You, Lord, so I'm just not going to say anything."

This is a lesson we need to learn. You can't be transparent heedless of the company. When you give voice to what's hurting, to all of your pain, God knows your heart and your desires. But if wicked people hear you, even if you say it with good intentions, they will take that and twist and turn it into some sort of argument against our God and against the truth. So, we must be careful where we are transparent and unveil the pain, the hurt that we're feeling. *I will guard my mouth with a muzzle, so long as the wicked are in my presence.*

Charles Spurgeon said, "Unguarded ways are generally unholy ones. Heedless is another word for graceless. If a man's own children rail at him, no wonder if his enemies' mouths are full of abuse."[7] He is drawing an analogy between that man's children who would rail at their father, and us, if we rail at God. If the children rail at him, don't be surprised when the father's enemies rail at him also. We don't want to be guilty of encouraging our father's enemies to rail at him, so let us, as his children, not rail at him or be misunderstood to be thought of as railing at him. David said, "I'm going to put a guard over my speech." This is a commitment that he made, but he finds it to be **a challenging commitment.**

Verse 2: *I was mute and silent;* literally, "I held my peace to no avail." "I held my peace from good" is the idea. It's difficult to know exactly what he has in mind. The NET Bible has, *I was stone silent; I held back the urge to speak. My frustration grew worse.* The ESV continues verse 2, *and my distress grew worse.*

---

[7] Charles Spurgeon, *The Treasury of David* on Psalm 39:1.

David was challenged by an inner turmoil, something going on in his mind and heart. We don't know the specifics, but one thing is clear from this Psalm. David saw himself as under the disciplining hand of God (vs.10,11 &13).

Look at verses 10-11: *Remove your stroke from me; I am spent by the hostility of your hand. When you discipline a man with rebukes for sin, you consume like a moth what is dear to him; surely all mankind is a mere breath!* Then he says in verse 13: *Look away from me, that I may smile again....* David understands that he is being disciplined by God. The hostile stroke has come from the hand of God, but David has determined not to sin by talking about it. However, his pain is increasing while his frustration and distress are pent up within him.

God has designed a way for us to be relieved from pain by expressing ourselves. We just need to be wise about how we do it, and that's what David does. Verse 3: *My heart became hot within me. As I mused, the fire burned; then I spoke with my tongue:* His inner man was aflame with bothersome thoughts, so he broke his silence. He did it in a wise and God-honoring way by taking these thoughts to God in prayer.

David's First Request

Instead of voicing his thoughts before the wicked, <u>he wisely goes to the Lord</u>. Verse 4: *O LORD,* so, he's not saying this to others. He's not saying this in the presence of the wicked. This is David now before the Lord, and he's going to unburden his soul.

If you feel burdened, troubled or your heart has been burning within you, can I encourage you to do the same?

Have you been disciplining yourself saying, "I know that God loves me, and I reverence Him, and I don't want to sin against Him. So, I'm just not going to talk about what's bothering me." I want to encourage you to unburden your soul, but to do it wisely. There are godly people you can share your burden with, but the first and primary place to go for unburdening your soul is before the Lord Himself.

That's what David does here, and he does it with a **very wise request**. This is the pattern I mentioned earlier: request, then reflection. You see the request in verse 4, and the reflection in verses 5 and 6. **Here's his request**: *O LORD, make me know my end and what is the measure of my days; let me know how fleeting I am!* He asks God to reveal to him just how short his life really is—how fleeting or transient he is. He wants God to help him understand his mortality and the brevity of his life.

Now someone might say, "Well, David, to ask for such a thing means that you already grasp it." And indeed, to some degree he did. If we understand David to simply be saying, "Let me know intellectually that my life is not going to be very long," we will have misunderstood him. That's not what he's saying. When he says, *Make me know my end*, I think he means, "Lord, let this reality not just be information to me, not just be in my mind, but let me now live in light of such a reality." David is saying, I realize my frailty, now help me to know how to live in this condition. Teach me a heart of wisdom in light of the brevity of my life. Verse 4— "Let me daily practice a life that reflects the knowledge of these realities and how fleeting I am." You see the same thing in Psalm 90:12, when Moses wrote, *So teach us to number our days that we may get a heart of wisdom.*

As I said earlier, when you treat temporal things like they're eternal things, that's foolishness. Wisdom means recognizing the brevity of life so that you make the right use of it instead of wasting it. "Teach me that, Lord." Are you making the best use of your life? Have you, like David, acknowledged and embraced the truth that your life is not going to last very long? And are you asking God, in light of that reality, to teach you how to make the best use of your days?

In verse 5, **David now reflects on the brevity of life, beginning with his own.** *Behold, you have made my days a few handbreadths, and my lifetime is as nothing before you.* His reflection begins with his own life. He's thinking that his life is like an apparition, a ghost-like existence. He says, *My life is but a few handbreadths.* "Handbreath" is a term of measurement, the width of four fingers, a little over two inches. David says his life is just a few of them.

Notice that he recognizes it is sovereign GOD who set the boundaries for man's existence. Our average lifespan of 70 years is not dictated by impersonal forces like nature or science. He says, "You have made my days like this." God is the One who set the boundaries for the time of human existence. Do you realize that? In the next statement he compares his *lifetime* to the eternal nature of God. *My lifetime is as nothing before You.* You're eternal. My life on this earth, as I am right now, is brief. It's nothing.

Seeing himself as nothing before God leads him to recognize his smallness. It's a good lesson. Men want to believe that they're a big deal. We tend to think, in some sense, the world didn't exist until we were born, and in some sense, that the world will cease to exist if we're gone. But the truth, as you know from God's Word, is that the world existed before us, and if the Lord tarries, this world will exist after us. We're here for just a few handbreadths, that's all. We're not really a big deal, just a vapor.

We see in verse 6 that David doesn't stop at thinking about himself, but wisely reflects on a larger picture, that of all mankind. *Surely all mankind stands as a mere breath!— all mankind*. And since *Selah* may mean "pause" (we're not certain that it does), stop and let that sink in.

Surely all mankind stands as a mere breath! Surely a man goes about as a shadow! David compares man's life to a ghost or an apparition; he seems real, but he's like a phantom, a shadow—here for a moment and then gone.

And yet, here's the foolishness of it all, next statement: *Surely for nothing they are in turmoil; man heaps up wealth and does not know who will gather!* People are in turmoil for nothing—for a breath, for a shadow. Man doesn't understand this. He lives this <u>shadowy life</u> as if it is <u>substance</u>. What do these men do with this little bit of time that they have? They spend it in an uproar, chasing after things, trying to accumulate all they can, but these things are just as much a vapor as they are. Instead of setting his heart on eternity, on what is substantive, what will last forever, this shadowy existence called man sets his heart, his energies and his concerns on things that won't last. <u>They are in turmoil for nothing</u>.

How much of what <u>you're</u> spending your days on will amount to nothing? How much of where you focus your thoughts, your energies, your concerns, and even your troubled heart, will amount to nothing? Do you notice what men will sell for things that won't last forever? They'll sell their marriage and time with their children for things that won't last forever. They'll even sell their soul. Listen to what our Lord said, *What will it profit a man if he gains the whole world and forfeits his soul?* (Matt. 16:26) What will it profit him? Nothing.

During his lifetime, man heaps up riches that he cannot keep, and he doesn't even know who is going to have them. Someone might object at this point and say, "Oh yes, I do. I know who is going to have them. My kids and grandkids are going to have them. Can I tell you, my friend, that <u>you don't know that?</u> You don't know what the future will hold. You may think you know, but you don't, and you won't be around to know. How many people thought they left their children a good inheritance, but it ended up being wasted? Many people in the history of the world have seen what they worked so hard for, gone in an instant, shortly after they entered eternity. You just don't know.

Proverbs 23:4 says this: *Do not toil to acquire wealth; be discerning enough to desist. When your eyes light on it, it is gone, for suddenly it sprouts wings, flying like an eagle toward heaven.*

So, we have a conflict of perspectives, don't we? God says, "It's not worth much;" the world says, "It's worth everything." Now, who are you going to believe? God says, "It's not worth much;" the world says, "It's worth your soul." Who are you going to believe?

A Confession Worked Out While in Distress

Verse 7 begins the second section of this psalm, and in it we find a confession, which is the psalm's high point. In David's commitment we discover that he isn't irreverent nor disloyal. He's struggling with some honest questions.

Similarly, **in his confession, we find that in spite of his difficulties, his hope is in the Lord.** This man trusts the Lord.

Verse 7: *And now, O Lord, for what do I wait?*— "In this lifespan that is like a shadow, in this world full of shadows, things that don't last, what do I grab onto for something substantive? "

My hope is in You. In this transitory world, there is someone in whom is found eternal hope and endless pleasures. Do you want to hold onto something substantive? Embrace the Lord, the living God. If you want to live for something, for someone who is going to give you that which lasts forever, <u>then set your heart on the living God.</u> "I trust in You. I wait for You. My hope is in You."

As you listen to David working this out, hear it in its context. This is a man who trusts the Lord. This is so helpful for believers, because as we come face to face with the brutal realities of life, we still struggle with the difficulties of life in a world that's under a curse.

David's Second Request

His second request is found in verse 8: *Deliver me from all my transgressions. Do not make me the scorn of the fool!*

What's he asking for? **"Lord, would You have mercy upon me?"** Whatever he's going through, he has connected it to his sins. He's afraid that his life will end up on the trash heap of testimonies, that his life will become a point for mocking among the wicked, among the fools. So, he's saying, "Lord, would You save me from what I've done to myself? Would You have mercy upon me?"

Do you know that if the Lord should count iniquities, no one could stand? From this verse we are able to see a need for greater humility. Do you know what we do sometimes? We look at the so-called fallen and with proud hearts say, "Look at them." It's as if we have escaped that condition on our own, as if the reason why our life is not on the trash heap of testimonies is because we're so wise and good and obedient.

To say it another way, how many of your sins, if the Lord had let each sin run its full course, could have ruined you? How many of your acts of disobedience could have ruined you? Do you think you stand on your own? If any man thinks he stands, what should he do? Take heed lest he fall. "O Lord, have mercy upon me. Save me from myself. Save me from my transgressions. Deliver me from them. Don't make me the scorn of the fool. Don't let my life end up as fodder for fools." David understands the potential for his transgressions to ruin the rest of his life.

Just as he's done before, following a request, David now offers a reflection, and it's a submissive reflection. Verse 9: *I am mute; I do not open my mouth, for it is you who have done it.* He is in no position to complain about his present circumstances. They are from the hand of the Lord, and he's talking to God about them. So, even as he vents his desire to not be made a mockery as a result of his own transgressions, he leaves it in the hands of God. "I'm asking You to deliver me, but I know this: You are in control of what I'm experiencing right now. This is Your choice, and I have no right to complain. I ask You to keep me from being the fodder for fools, but Lord, I have no right to open my mouth. You're the One who has me under Your hand. It is Your right to do it, and what You do is right. So, I don't want to complain sinfully. I have no right to complain." That is a submissive way to think.

David's Third Request

David's final request comes in verse 10: *Remove your stroke from me; I am spent by the hostility of your hand.* "Save me from myself. If You choose not to, I can't utter a word. I'm under Your sovereign hand, **but I ask You to lift this plague from me, to lift Your hand of discipline from me because I'm spent by it.**" He leaves it in the God's hand, but he can ask for God to lift his hand. David is giving voice to his smallness. God has given him a stroke, or as the NASB translates it, a plague.

David says he is spent by the hostility, or opposition of God's hand. The word translated *spent* means to be at a complete end, to be finished. He has come to the end of something. That is to say, "Lord, I don't feel like I can take anymore. I feel like I'm about to perish. I can't take anymore. If you choose not to, I can't complain, but Lord, would You lift Your hand?"

And then here's his reflection, verse 11: *When you discipline a man with rebukes for sin, you consume like a moth what is dear to him; surely all mankind is a mere breath!* He says, in effect, **"When You discipline a man with rebukes for sin, it's like a moth that consumes. This is what it feels like, Lord. Your hand is on me, and it seems like everything that is dear to me is disappearing, and I can't do anything about it. All mankind is just a mere breath before you.** You're big; I'm small. You're strong; I'm weak. You're eternal; I'm a breath."

So, when God begins to deal with a man, he has no chance. Do you want to know the foolishness of men? It is when they think they can fight against God and win. God can, and often does, systematically take away everything that man counts dear. My friend, if the Lord sets His hand against you, you have no chance.

Pleas for Mercy

So, what do you do? What do you do when you feel like you're under the disciplining hand of God and everything dear to you is being consumed? You know that it's your own doing, but you can't open your mouth in complaint. God is the One who has you in this place. What do you do? What does David do?

Verse 12: *Hear my prayer, O LORD, and give ear to my cry; hold not your peace at my tears! For I am a sojourner with you, a guest, like all my fathers. Look away from me, that I may smile again, before I depart and am no more!*

What do you do? Like David, **you cry out to God for mercy with a humble, submissive, believing heart.** And you do it in a way that recognizes the character of the God whom you're addressing. When David says, *Give ear to my cry, hold not your peace at my tears!* what does he know about God? God doesn't remain silent and unmoved when there are sincere, humble, heartbroken tears. "Lord, see my tears and don't be silent. I'm appealing to Your compassionate heart. **Have compassion upon me.**"

He appeals to the grace of God. When he says, *I am a sojourner with you, a guest, like all my fathers*, **he's talking about his relationship to the Lord**, and he's tying his own relationship to God with that of his forefathers. There's a history here. David's forefathers were specifically chosen by God, but not by anything of their own merit (Deut. 7:6-7). And like a sojourner, a guest, he has a relationship with

God that he can't claim by nature. He is not someone who can claim to have rights to exist in the presence of God. This is something God has afforded. **This is something God has given, granted, and it's a matter of grace.** "In many ways, Lord, I'm still like a stranger in my knowledge of You. I stand where I stand with You because of Your grace. You've allowed me this place and position with You. O Lord, remember me." While we are in this part of our journey (our sojourning), we see in a glass dimly. One day we will see face to face.

You don't stand before the Lord on the basis of your works, do you? So, when you find yourself under the disciplining hand of God, do you want to appeal to Him on the basis of your works, or do you want to appeal to His grace? "Lord, have compassion upon me, and be gracious to me."

He cries out for one more thing—for relief, for blessing. *Look away from me.* Obviously, he doesn't mean "forget me." What he means is, "Lord, You're giving Your attention to me in the form of discipline, to me, this small breath of a person, this shadow. You've set your attention on me in the form of discipline. Would You please look away from me? Would you allow me to smile again *before I depart and am no more*? Would You let me know Your favor in a fresh way before my life is over?"

In his dilemma, David has rightly cried out to the Lord, but a question for you to consider is, "Where are you going to fix your eyes?" David's cry is an honest one. He captures our feelings and asks for forgiveness.

So, you have cried out to God for His compassion, His grace, His favor and His blessing, but what will you focus on? James Boice puts it well. "Instead of just focusing on where God places His eyes, we need to concern ourselves where we place ours."[8] Often, what is missing from our perspective when we are in the midst of great pain, is a firm commitment to keep our eyes fixed on our God while we trust His wise dealings with us.

If God's eyes are fixed on us in the form of discipline, are we convinced that He loves us? If we're His people, does He love us? Is God as concerned about your happiness as He is your holiness? And so, if He's at work disciplining you as a son, even though it's unpleasant at times, don't you know that His goal is His glory and your good? So you remain under the trial, fixing your eyes on the Author and the Perfecter of your faith (Heb. 12:1-2). David expresses that in a sense in verse 7 when he says, *And now, O LORD, for what do I wait? My hope is in You.* And yet, he asks God for relief.

Conclusion

Have you been living in Psalm 39 in terms of your feelings? Have you been brought face-to-face, with the brevity and difficulty of life, with your own mortality? Would you say to the Lord, "God, grant me a heart of wisdom to know what to do with this, to make the most of this life that You grant me"?

And if what you're feeling is due to your own sins, would you confess them and turn from them? If you've been in turmoil running after that which you can't keep, would you accept what the rich young ruler rejected?[9] Jesus

---

[8] James Montgomery Boice, *Psalms Volume 1: Psalms 1-41* (An Expositional Commentary Grand Rapids: Baker Books, 2005)

[9] See Matthew 19:16-22.

offered him treasure in heaven if he would throw it all away and follow Christ. He said no, but would you say yes? Would you throw away the shadows you've been chasing after? Would you throw them away to follow Jesus right now?

Would you set your heart on what is treasure indeed? Would you stop listening to the testimony of the world, which says all these shadows are really important? Would you listen to the testimony of God instead? Would you stop trading everlasting pleasures for that which keeps running away from you and doesn't ultimately satisfy you, but leaves you empty? And it will continue to leave you empty for the rest of your life. Would you recognize that? Would you repent and cast yourself on the mercy of God, saying, "If you don't grant this, I can't say a word, but I appeal to Your compassion and to Your grace, and I ask for Your blessing"?

God doesn't ignore your tears. In fact, this God, the Almighty God, gives you a promise:

Jeremiah 29:13 *You will seek me and find me, when you seek me with all your heart.*

Psalm 23

The Lord Is My Shepherd

PSALM 23

A Psalm of David

[1] The LORD is my shepherd; I shall not want.
[2]   He makes me lie down in green pastures.
He leads me beside still waters.
[3]   He restores my soul.
He leads me in paths of righteousness for his name's sake.

[4] Even though I walk through the valley of the shadow of death,
    I will fear no evil,
for you are with me;
    your rod and your staff,
    they comfort me.

[5] You prepare a table before me
    in the presence of my enemies;
you anoint my head with oil;
    my cup overflows.

[6] Surely goodness and mercy shall follow me all the days of my life,
    and I shall dwell in the house of the LORD forever.

Familiarity with something is often good, but at times it causes a negative effect. For example, we can be married for a number of years, and before long we can forget what a blessing we have in our spouse. After a while we can forget what a blessing it is to have our children, or we forget what a blessing our parents are to us. We forget what a blessing our job is, until it's not there anymore. There are so many areas where, sadly, we come to realize that. By becoming familiar and comfortable with something, we have missed the beauty and the blessing and the wonder of it.

Perhaps the saddest example of all is that we do this with God. We are familiar with His blessings, and we begin to take them for granted. We are familiar with portions of His Word, and unfortunately, we can begin to read those portions with such a familiarity that we miss their beauty.

I think Psalm 23 is an example of this. It is perhaps the most well-known passage in all of the Old Testament. It's often read and quoted, even by unbelievers in certain situations and settings. And if we're not careful, we end up just skimming over it, speeding through it. We begin to automatically recall the things we already know and have heard about it, and we miss the fact that there are fresh treasures to be gathered every time we come to these verses.

I encourage you not to fall prey to that error, but to consider this Psalm afresh and anew. Right now, before we begin to look at it, ask the Lord to speak to your heart in a refreshing, new way through what He has recorded here in Psalm 23 about Himself and His relationship to us.

This psalm is ascribed to David and we'll begin by focusing on the opening statement, *The LORD is my shepherd.* "The Lord is my shepherd."

An astounding statement

This is an astounding statement, a statement that not just anyone can make. It is truly astounding that the self-existent God Who made everything, Who sustains everything, Who owns everything, and Who needs nothing, would concern Himself with creatures like us. The thought that God would shepherd you, would make you an individual object of His care and concern, and would own you as His, the way that a shepherd personally relates to one of his sheep, is an astounding thought.

There are many images used in the Old Testament to talk about God's relationship to His people. He is a King, a Ruler, and a Deliverer. In more impersonal terms, He is a Rock, a Shield and a Fortress. But David, who knew what it was to be a shepherd, chooses this most intimate term when he says, *The LORD is my shepherd*. To the sheep, his shepherd is everything. He lives with his flock and knows his flock. The shepherd is their guide and the one who leads them to food and drink. He is, in that sense, their provider, their protector and He is their physician—their everything. And David says, "He, the Lord God, is my shepherd."

In fact, it would be an arrogant thought to claim that God is your Shepherd if God Himself had not revealed this sort of intimate relationship with His people, but He has. It was David who acknowledged the wonder of God's concern with mankind in general when he said to the Lord twice, "What is man, that You would think of us? What is man that You concern Yourself with us?" Consider the opening verses of Psalms 8 and 144, psalms of David:

Psalm 8 *O LORD, our Lord,*
  how majestic is your name in all the earth!
You have set your glory above the heavens.

2 Out of the mouth of babies and infants,
you have established strength because of your foes,
*   to still the enemy and the avenger.*

3 When I look at your heavens, the work of your fingers,
*   the moon and the stars, which you have set in place,*
4 what is man that you are mindful of him,
*   and the son of man that you care for him?"*

Psalm 144 *Blessed be the LORD, my rock,*
*   who trains my hands for war,*
*   and my fingers for battle;*
2 he is my steadfast love and my fortress,
*   my stronghold and my deliverer,*
my shield and he in whom I take refuge,
*   who subdues peoples under me.*

3 O LORD, what is man that you regard him,
*   or the son of man that you think of him?"*

If it is astounding that God should concern Himself with mankind as a whole, then isn't it even more astounding to say that God concerns Himself with me? That He is my shepherd? And yet, David recognizes that God takes an individual interest in him. Consider what he says in the first 18 verses of Psalm 139.

Psalm 139: A Psalm of David

1 O LORD, you have searched me and known me!
2 You know when I sit down and when I rise up;
*   you discern my thoughts from afar.*
3 You search out my path and my lying down
*   and are acquainted with all my ways.*
4 Even before a word is on my tongue,
*   behold, O LORD, you know it altogether.*
5 You hem me in, behind and before,

and lay your hand upon me.
⁶ Such knowledge is too wonderful for me;
    it is high; I cannot attain it.

⁷ Where shall I go from your Spirit?
    Or where shall I flee from your presence?
⁸ If I ascend to heaven, you are there!
    If I make my bed in Sheol, you are there!
⁹ If I take the wings of the morning
    and dwell in the uttermost parts of the sea,
¹⁰ even there your hand shall lead me,
    and your right hand shall hold me.
¹¹ If I say, "Surely the darkness shall cover me,
    and the light about me be night,"
¹² even the darkness is not dark to you;
    the night is bright as the day,
    for darkness is as light with you.

¹³ For you formed my inward parts;
    you knitted me together in my mother's womb.
¹⁴ I praise you, for I am fearfully and wonderfully made.
Wonderful are your works;
    my soul knows it very well.
¹⁵ My frame was not hidden from you,
when I was being made in secret,
    intricately woven in the depths of the earth.
¹⁶ Your eyes saw my unformed substance;
in your book were written, every one of them,
    the days that were formed for me,
    when as yet there was none of them.

¹⁷ How precious to me are your thoughts, O God!
    How vast is the sum of them!
¹⁸ If I would count them, they are more than the sand.
    I awake, and I am still with you.

Do you understand that the wonder is not just that Almighty God would concern Himself with <u>mankind</u>, but the astounding truth that Almighty <u>God would be an individual human being's shepherd</u>? This is an astounding statement, "The Lord is my shepherd."

A searching statement

Second, not only is it an astounding statement; it's **a searching statement**. One of the reasons why this psalm gets quoted even by unbelievers, is because its words are so comforting. But maybe it is comforting to them because they rush past the first line without thinking about it. David doesn't say, "The Lord is <u>our</u> shepherd;" he says, *The LORD is <u>my</u> shepherd.*

What David writes here is true of every genuine believer, but the Lord is not everyone's shepherd, in the sense that He's David's shepherd in this Psalm. And so, right away, when David is giving this personal testimony as it were, *The LORD is my shepherd,* the question must be asked: "Can <u>you</u> truthfully say what David writes here? Can <u>you</u> truthfully say that the Lord is <u>your</u> shepherd? Do <u>you</u> have that saving relationship to Almighty God? Have <u>your</u> sins been forgiven? Have <u>you</u> looked to God for the provision that He has made and ordained for the forgiveness of <u>your</u> sins, and a right standing before Him?"

David knew the joy of forgiveness and the joy of redemption. This is a redeemed man; thus, he is able to say, *The LORD is my shepherd,* but you can't know the Lord as your Shepherd until you know the Lord as your Redeemer. The Lord is not your Shepherd unless Jesus is your Savior.

The New Testament makes this plain. The wonder of wonders is that the Shepherd, God Himself, stepped out of heaven and came to this earth. The good Shepherd, the great Shepherd of the sheep, the chief Shepherd, the everlasting Shepherd, the Shepherd of forgiven ones, came from heaven to earth, was born of a virgin, and lived a sinless life, dying on a cross, to lay down His life for the sheep, and was raised from the dead. He did all this to bring men to God, to seek and save the lost, so that His sheep would hear His voice and follow Him. He did this so that <u>there would be one flock with one Shepherd</u>. This is why Jesus came into the world, to save His sheep. And so, if Jesus is not your Savior, then you're not one of His sheep, and the Lord is not your shepherd.

Jesus referred to Himself as the GOOD SHEPHERD in John 10:11, *I am the <u>good shepherd</u>. The good shepherd lays down his life for the sheep.* Just a few verses later (10:14-16), He said, *I am the good shepherd. I know my own and my own know me, just as the Father knows me and I know the Father; and I lay down my life for the sheep. And I have other sheep that are not of this fold.*—Speaking there of Gentile believers who would be gathered in— *I must bring them also, and they will listen to my voice. So there will be one flock, one shepherd.* Jesus is the good shepherd.

Jesus is also the GREAT SHEPHERD:

Hebrews 13:20 *Now may the God of peace who brought again from the dead our Lord Jesus, the <u>great shepherd</u> of the sheep, by the blood of the eternal covenant, [21] equip you with everything good that you may do his will, working in us that which is pleasing in his sight, through Jesus Christ, to whom be glory forever and ever. Amen*

Notice that Hebrews does not say here that God has done this <u>by</u> the great Shepherd, but that it is being done <u>through</u> the great Shepherd, through Jesus Christ. *To Him be glory forever and ever.* This is what we do as the church. We love and worship and adore and glorify our great Shepherd.

In the New Testament, elders are reminded that though they have a high, lofty privilege to serve the church as under-shepherds, with a weighty, sobering responsibility to watch for souls, we <u>all</u> wait for the chief Shepherd who is the good Shepherd, who is the great Shepherd, the Lord Jesus.

In a sense, this is what David is doing in Psalm 23. It was not uncommon for kings to be pictured in terms of a shepherd when it came to ruling their subjects. David is a king, and yet he acknowledges the power behind the throne. This king, to whom others might have looked to as a shepherd, says, *The Lord is my shepherd.*

The apostle Peter refers to Jesus as the CHIEF SHEPHERD:

1 Peter 5:1 *So I exhort the elders among you, as a fellow elder and a witness of the sufferings of Christ, as well as a partaker in the glory that is going to be revealed: [2] shepherd the flock of God that is among you, exercising oversight, not under compulsion, but willingly, as God would have you; not for shameful gain, but eagerly; [3] not domineering over those in your charge, but being examples to the flock. [4] And when the <u>chief Shepherd</u> appears, you will receive the unfading crown of glory.*

That's the goal of every good under-shepherd, to be an example to the flock and shepherd them in a way that is completely in keeping with the character of the chief Shepherd, so that one day when the He appears, the under-shepherd will hear "Well done."

Jesus is the EVERLASTING SHEPHERD:

Revelation 7:13-17 *Then one of the elders addressed me, saying, "Who are these, clothed in white robes, and from where have they come?"* [14] *I said to him, "Sir, you know." And he said to me, "These are the ones coming out of the great tribulation. They have washed their robes and made them white in the blood of the Lamb.*

[15] *Therefore they are before the throne of God,
    and serve him day and night in his temple;
    and he who sits on the throne will shelter them with
his presence.*
[16] *They shall hunger no more, neither thirst anymore;
    the sun shall not strike them,
    nor any scorching heat.*
[17] *For the Lamb in the midst of the throne will be their
<u>shepherd</u>,
    and he will guide them to springs of living water,
and God will wipe away every tear from their eyes."*

Isn't it good to know that He's not just our Shepherd <u>now</u>, but that He is our Shepherd <u>forever</u>! Jesus is the good Shepherd, the great Shepherd, the chief Shepherd, the everlasting Shepherd. Remember, He is not your Shepherd unless He has forgiven your sins; unless you have looked to Him and His sacrifice on the cross for the forgiveness of your sins, He is not your Shepherd. Jesus is the forgiven ones' Shepherd.

1 Peter 2:24 *He himself bore our sins in his body on the tree, that we might die to sin and live to righteousness. By his wounds you have been healed.* [25] *For you were straying like sheep, but have now returned to the <u>Shepherd</u> and Overseer of your souls.*

How has your return happened? How did you return to Shepherd and Overseer of your soul? Through the suffering of God's only Son. It was accomplished through His wounds, and by them you have been healed, forgiven, redeemed, and saved.

So, we have observed that *The LORD is my shepherd* is an astounding statement, and at the same time, a searching statement. Can you really say that the Lord your Shepherd? Do you know Him in salvation? Is Jesus your Savior? For if Christ is not your Savior, the Lord is not your Shepherd.

A comforting statement

Third, this is also **a comforting statement**. Who is your Shepherd? Yahweh. Who is your Shepherd, David? "The Lord is my Shepherd. Almighty God is my Shepherd." Does your thinking reflect that truth the way that it should? Do your emotions reflect a true understanding of that truth, that the Lord God is your Shepherd? Do your fears, anxieties, worries, and doubts reveal that you struggle with comprehending that no mere man is your Shepherd; but that the living God is your Shepherd?

Stop, and let it sink in—the One who is ALWAYS PRESENT, is your Shepherd. As we saw in Psalm 139:1-18, can you flee from His presence? David asked that question, didn't he? "Where can I go?" If you go to heaven, He's there. If you go to Sheol, He's there. If you take the wings of the morning and go out to the uttermost regions of the sea, He's there. So near to you that when you awake, He's there. His hand is upon you. His thoughts toward you are so vast that the sum of them outnumbers the sands on the seashore. This is your Shepherd, THE EVER-PRESENT ONE. The ALL-POWERFUL ONE is your Shepherd, the One who possesses all power, all authority.

Is there anything too difficult for the Lord? He is your Shepherd, THE ONE WHO IS PERFECTLY WISE.

If you say to yourself, "How will this work out? Where is this situation headed? Where will my deliverance come from? Who will be my helper? When will the circumstances change?" Take comfort, child of God, your situation is in the hand of God, and HE IS ALL-WISE. When He's ready to act, He will. He'll always act rightly, perfectly, and right on time. THE ONE WHO IS PERFECT LOVE, who loves you perfectly, is your Shepherd. YOUR SHEPHERD IS A WARRIOR, THE ONE WHO IS NEVER DEFEATED.

You may say, "But pastor, we have a great enemy in this world. He's roaming about like a lion seeking whom he may devour." Well, that's right. And we're told to be sober and alert. But make no mistake about it —we're in the hand of God, and no one is able to snatch us out. The evil one cannot touch us in the sense of destroying us, if we really have the Lord as our Shepherd. He's a warrior never defeated, the one who conquered the devil and the grave. This warrior is your shepherd.

He is THE ONE FULL OF COMPASSION. Does He really know what you're going through? Does He really know how you feel? Does He care about how you feel? In Luke 7 we see Jesus resurrecting the only son of a widow.

Luke 7:13 *And when the Lord saw her, he had compassion on her and said to her, "Do not weep." ¹⁴ Then he came up and touched the bier, and the* bearers *stood still. And he said, "Young man, I say to you, arise."*

We serve the God who really cares. This is your Shepherd, THE ONE WHO IS A FAITHFUL FATHER TO US, who disciplines and scourges every son whom He receives. He is the One who disciplines us, although it's not always pleasant right now, but it yields the peaceable fruit of righteousness. He's forming the character of His Son in us, and He's doing it perfectly. This is your Shepherd, THE ONE WHO CREATED EVERYTHING, SUSTAINS EVERYTHING, OWNS EVERYTHING, CONTROLS EVERYTHING. This is your Shepherd. The Lord is my Shepherd. How can anyone who can truly make this statement ever be afraid?

David wrote in Psalm 27: *The LORD is my light and my salvation; whom shall I fear? The LORD is the stronghold of my life; of whom shall I be afraid? When evildoers assail me to eat up my flesh, my adversaries and foes, it is they who stumble and fall. Though an army encamp against me, my heart shall not fear; though war arise against me, yet I will be confident.*

How can you say this, David? "Because the Lord is my Shepherd."

A submissive statement

Fourth, *The LORD is my Shepherd* is **a submissive statement** on the part of David. As I mentioned, shepherd analogies were not uncommon in the ancient world. They normally pictured the ruler, the king as the shepherd. But here David is saying that <u>he has</u> a shepherd, which is to say, <u>he needs</u> a shepherd.

Dear friend, do <u>you</u> need a shepherd? Do you recognize your need for God, so that you live your life humbly before Him, acknowledging your dependence upon Him, willfully, joyfully submitted to Him? It's a life where you say, "Not my will be done, but Yours, for You are all-wise, perfectly loving; You know what's best. The Lord is my shepherd.

I'm just a sheep. I need guidance. I need protection. I need provision. I need healing. I need a shepherd, and the Lord is my shepherd."

I love David's attitude expressed in the Book of 2 Samuel, chapter 7. Verses 8-13 contain the message to David given by God to the prophet, Nathan. It tells of all the wonderful blessings God has for him and the people of Israel, including that the Lord will establish the throne of his kingdom forever. This looks beyond anything fulfilled in Solomon. This looks to the Lord Jesus. Verse 14 says, *I will be to him a father, and he shall be to me a son.*—You have the mixture of images here, Solomon and the future Messiah, because of what is said next: "*When he commits iniquity, I will discipline him with the rod of men, with the stripes of the sons of men, *[15]* but my steadfast love will not depart from him, as I took it from Saul, whom I put away from before you. *[16]* And your house and your kingdom shall be made sure forever before me. Your throne shall be established forever.*" *[17]* In accordance with all these words, and in accordance with all this vision, Nathan spoke to David.*

Following is David's response:

[18] Then King David went in and sat before the Lord and said, "Who am I, O Lord GOD, and what is my house, that you have brought me thus far? *[19]* And yet this was a small thing in your eyes, O Lord GOD. You have spoken also of your servant's house for a great while to come, and this is instruction for mankind, O Lord GOD! *[20]* And what more can David say to you? For you know your servant, O Lord GOD! *[21]* Because of your promise, and according to your own heart, you have brought about all this greatness, to make your servant know it. *[22]* Therefore you are great, O*

LORD God. For there is none like you, and there is no God besides you, according to all that we have heard with our ears. [23] And who is like your people Israel, the one nation on earth whom God went to redeem to be his people, making himself a name and doing for them great and awesome things by driving out before your people, whom you redeemed for yourself from Egypt, a nation and its gods? [24] And you established for yourself your people Israel to be your people forever. And you, O LORD, became their God. [25] And now, O Lord GOD, confirm forever the word that you have spoken concerning your servant and concerning his house, and do as you have spoken. [26] And your name will be magnified forever, saying, 'The LORD of hosts is God over Israel,' and the house of your servant David will be established before you. [27] For you, O LORD of hosts, the God of Israel, have made this revelation to your servant, saying, 'I will build you a house.' Therefore your servant has found courage to pray this prayer to you. [28] And now, O Lord GOD, you are God, and your words are true, and you have promised this good thing to your servant. [29] Now therefore may it please you to bless the house of your servant, so that it may continue forever before you. For you, O Lord GOD, have spoken, and with your blessing shall the house of your servant be blessed forever."

After David hears the Lord's promises through Nathan, David magnifies the Lord for what he has determined to do. But with respect to himself, his attitude is, "Who am I? What is my house that You would bring me this far, and that You would promise these great things to me?" This is not how kings normally think. It is a gracious, humble attitude.

So, when you say, *The LORD is my shepherd*, <u>it should be, it must be</u>, with a heart of humility and submission. The humble attitude is the <u>accurate</u> attitude, where you see yourself rightly. Only a fool is wise in his own eyes. The humble attitude is a <u>wise</u> attitude, therefore, it's a <u>gracious</u> attitude. Men by nature are sinfully proud, and only the Lord can teach you humility. A humble attitude is a <u>blessed</u> attitude. God blesses the humble.

Proverbs 3:33-35 says: *The LORD's curse is on the house of the wicked, but he blesses the dwelling of the righteous. Toward the scorners he is scornful, but to the humble he gives favor. The wise will inherit honor, but fools get disgrace.*

Psalm 138:6 says: *For though the LORD is exalted, yet he regards the lowly, but the haughty he knows from afar.*

Jesus said in **Matthew 23:12**, *Whoever exalts himself shall be humbled, and whoever humbles himself shall be exalted.*

1 Peter 5:5 *You younger men, likewise be subject to the elders. All of you, clothe yourselves with humility toward one another, for "God is opposed to the proud but gives grace to the humble."*

Here in Psalm 23 we find a picture of a powerful king whose attitude was, **"Who am I? The Lord is my shepherd."**

I ask you, is He <u>your</u> Shepherd? Are you astounded by the fact that He is? Is it true that He is? Do you take comfort in the knowledge that your Shepherd is God? Or, do you live your life in the type of fear that says you haven't understood that? And, are you submitted to Him, ready to do whatever He wants, knowing that on behalf of His people God graciously performs everything else that follows?

Everything else in Psalm 23 flows out of the statement. *The LORD is my shepherd*; therefore, you see, *I shall not want.* Therefore, *He makes me lie down in green pastures.*—along with all the rest of the blessings and provisions that follow. It all flows out of this one thought: The LORD is my shepherd.

A Survey of Riches

The Lord is my Shepherd. We have seen that this single statement describes a relationship with the Lord that is not only astounding, but also searching, comforting and submissive. Moving from this statement of relationship, we see next a survey of riches, the blessings that belong to those who can truly say that the Lord is their Shepherd. Everything that follows in this psalm flows from that, because it all depends on your relationship to Him. If the Lord is your Shepherd, then these things are true of you, just as surely as they were true of David. What does it mean to be shepherded by God?

Side note: God's under-shepherds

Before delving into the rest of the psalm, I want to point out that the Lord has established and ordained, human leaders to shepherd His people here on earth. This reveals God's commitment to care for them.

In 1 Peter 5:1-2, Peter writes, *So I exhort the elders among you, as a fellow elder and a witness of the sufferings of Christ, as well as a partaker in the glory that is going to be revealed: shepherd the flock of God that is among you....* This is the Holy Spirit, through Peter, saying to elders, "Shepherd My people." But ultimately, this is the revelation of the care and concern of the chief Shepherd, because verse 4 says, *And when the chief Shepherd appears, you will receive the unfading crown of glory....* If you shepherd the people of God well, there will be commendation for you, because the chief Shepherd cares about His people.

When the Lord restores Simon Peter in John 21, He says to Peter more than once, *"Simon, son of John, do you love*

Me?" He said to Him, "Yes, Lord. You know that I love you." He said to him, "Shepherd My sheep."

And in Acts 20:28, Paul writes to the Ephesian elders, *Be on guard for yourselves and for all the flock, among which the Holy Spirit has made you overseers, to shepherd the church of God....*

So, wherever you have these commandments given to human shepherds, it is a reflection of the Lord's shepherding care for us. One day, we will meet our Savior face to face, and will personally and directly experience His shepherding ministry.

Ezekiel tells of this:

Ezekiel 34:22 *I will rescue my flock; they shall no longer be a prey. And I will judge between sheep and sheep. ²³ And I will set up over them one shepherd, my servant David, and he shall feed them: he shall feed them and be their shepherd. ²⁴ And I, the LORD, will be their God, and my servant David shall be prince among them. I am the LORD; I have spoken.*

When the Lord is your Shepherd, you lack nothing.

So then, what is true if the Lord is your Shepherd? **You are rich, well-provided for, you lack nothing.** *The Lord is my shepherd; I shall not want.* The Hebrew word translated *want* here means to lack, to be without, to be in want. David says that because the Lord is his shepherd, he will not be in want. He will lack nothing.

Obviously, this doesn't mean that you have everything you would desire, or that you get just anything that you want. But it does mean that you lack nothing in terms of what you really need. When the Lord is your Shepherd, you can be <u>absolutely certain</u> that you will never lack what you really need. The Lord meets the needs of His people, faithfully, constantly, perfectly, and wisely.

That's a great assurance, isn't it? No matter what day it is we're facing, no matter what circumstances we're walking through, we can be assured that the Lord will meet our real needs—not our imagined needs, maybe not everything that we desire, but indeed, what we need.

This same word is used in Deuteronomy 2:7 when it says, *For the LORD your God has blessed you in all the work of your hands. He knows your going through this great wilderness. These forty years the Lord your God has been with you. You have <u>lacked</u> nothing.*

That helps us understand this statement in Psalm 23. We remember how God dealt with Israel as they wandered in the wilderness.[10] Sinfully, they weren't always satisfied with what the Lord provided, and they rarely got what they wanted. Think about those wilderness wanderings, about the complaining, and all the rest—those people never lacked what they needed. God met their needs.

In Matthew 6: 8 & 32, the good Shepherd is reminding us not to be anxious, not to flit about like pagans, trying to take care of ourselves, but to trust the Lord. Jesus reminds us, *"Your heavenly Father knows you need these things."* Food, clothing, and shelter—your heavenly Father knows you need these things, and He will meet your needs.

---

[10] Their 40 years of wandering are detailed in the books of Exodus, Leviticus, Numbers, and Deuteronomy.

Psalm 34:10 uses the same word: *The young lions do lack and suffer hunger; but they who seek the LORD shall not be* <u>*in want*</u> *of any good thing.*

God has chosen to take to Himself a family, a flock. He has bound Himself up with the welfare of that family and flock, so much so, that the Shepherd of that flock came into the world and gave His very life for the sheep. It is by His own blood that we are all provided for without any lack. *The LORD is my Shepherd; I shall not want.* I will lack nothing.

<u>When the Lord is your Shepherd, you are cared for.</u>

HE MAKES ME LIE DOWN IN GREEN PASTURES

Second: **When the Lord is your Shepherd, you are cared for**. *I shall not want. He makes me lie down in green pastures. He leads me beside still waters.* Notice that the Lord is actively involved in this. <u>He</u> makes David to lie down in green pastures. <u>He, God</u>, that is, leads David beside still waters. <u>God</u> restores his soul. <u>God</u> leads him in the paths of righteousness for the sake of <u>God's</u> name. Even today, God is active in the lives of His children, meeting needs not in some disconnected, impersonal kind of way, but meeting all of our needs in a very personal way, in a way where He is active in our lives.

It is because God is acting that we lack nothing. He causes us to lie down in green pastures. The word translated *green* there is a word that speaks of fresh grass, new grass, tender grass, the kind that would come up after a rain. It was a kind that would be found seasonally in the land of Israel, winter, and in the spring. Most of the time a shepherd would have to take his flock on long trips, migrating, looking for food and water. But the picture here is, when the Lord is your Shepherd you're stationed in places of fresh, tender vegetation, well fed, well taken care of.

The same word is used in 2 Samuel.

2 Samuel 23:3 where it says: *The God of Israel has spoken; the Rock of Israel has said to me: When one rules justly over men, ruling in the fear of God, ⁴ he dawns on them like the morning light, like the sun shining forth on a cloudless morning, like rain that makes <u>grass</u> to sprout from the earth."*

I've noticed this with my yard, maybe you have, too: I can water it and water it and water it, yet, if it rains, it just greens up.

Deuteronomy 32:2 also uses this word: *May my teaching drop as the rain, my speech distill as the dew, like gentle rain upon the <u>tender grass</u>, and like showers upon the herb.*

So, the idea is new, fresh, tender grass that has been watered by rain showers. *The Lord is my shepherd; I shall not lack. He makes me lie down in <u>green</u> pastures.*

What I'm saying to you, and what the Word of God is saying to us is, the Lord meets our needs, and He does it in a way that we experience goodness. He doesn't just provide the bare necessities. He takes care of us according to what He knows is best for us, and what He supplies is good. Green pastures—good provision.

There's a lesson for us here regarding our love for people and our desire to be good stewards of what God gives us as we take care of others. This could apply to a family or in any other way the Lord would use you to benefit someone else. Sometimes we think that being a good steward means that we just provide the barest of necessities, but that's not how our God deals with us. Our God delights to give His children good things. We are Shepherded by the God who delights in showing goodness to His sheep with rich, green, luscious pastures.

Deuteronomy speaks of His provision:

Deuteronomy 6:10 *And when the LORD your God brings you into the land that he swore to your fathers, to Abraham, to Isaac, and to Jacob, to give you—with great and good cities that you did not build, 11 and houses full of all good things that you did not fill, and cisterns that you did not dig, and vineyards and olive trees that you did not plant—and when you eat and are full, 12 then take care lest you forget the LORD, who brought you out of the land of Egypt, out of the house of slavery.*

A few years ago, there was a disagreement in US politics concerning the phrase, "You built that." One side said, "You didn't build that," claiming that everything depends on what the government has done. The other side said, "You did build that," claiming that individuals built everything. Both were wrong, because the government didn't build it, and you didn't build it. We work, but in the truest sense, in the final sense, the Lord built it. What is true of the nation of Israel is true of any nation—God is the One who supplies. And what is true of nations is true of individuals. Whatever you have, God gave it to you. And He delights to give good things.

Psalm 21 says: A Psalm of David. *O LORD, in your strength the king rejoices, and in your salvation how greatly he exults! You have given him his heart's desire and have not withheld the request of his lips. For you meet* *him with rich blessings; you set a crown of fine gold upon his head.*

The Lord Jesus reminds us in **Matthew 7** of the nature of our God when He says, *[7] Ask, and it will be given to you; seek, and you will find; knock, and it will be opened to you. [8] For everyone who asks receives, and the one who seeks finds, and to the one who knocks it will be opened. [9] Or which one of you, if his son asks him for bread, will give him a stone? [10] Or if he asks for a fish, will give him a serpent? [11] If you then, who are evil, know how to give good gifts to your children, how much more will your Father who is in heaven give good things to those who ask him!*

The Lord is my Shepherd; I shall not lack. I shall not want. He makes me lie down in green pastures.

HE LEADS ME BESIDE STILL WATERS

Next, we see that God's provision includes more than just luscious grass. Notice, *He leads me beside still waters.* The Hebrew word translated *still* means resting, or a resting place. **The emphasis here is not just a physical provision of water, but also a provision for the spirit, for the soul in terms of rest, tranquility, and peace.** *He makes me lie down*, you see. This rest takes place in green pastures. *He leads me beside still waters*—waters that are restful, quiet, tranquil, and placid. Rough, raging water would disturb the sheep, so that they could not drink from it in peace. The Lord meets that need and desire within us for peace and rest and safety.

Isaiah 28:11 *For by people of strange lips and with a foreign tongue the Lord will speak to this people, [12] to* *whom he has said, "This is rest; give rest to the weary; and this is repose"; yet they would not hear.*

God was willing to give rest to His people, but they often didn't want the rest that God offered.

The provision that David describes here goes beyond even physical and emotional provision. It extends to the chief way God cares for us, that is, to our inner man—our spiritual provision. He shepherds us in the food that He gives us, the grass that we enjoy, using the metaphor, and the water that we drink. It is sustenance found in His very Word. <u>The Lord feeds our souls, and in that way, He grants us rest and peace.</u>

Jeremiah 3:14 *Return, O faithless children, declares the LORD; for I am your master; I will take you, one from a city and two from a family, and I will bring you to Zion.* *[15] And I will give you shepherds after my own heart, who will feed you with knowledge and understanding.*

You see, God cares for His sheep by feeding them with knowledge and with truth. This is how the heart is refreshed. He feeds our soul and gives rest to our hearts through the ministry of His word.

In **Ezekiel 34**:1-24 you find one of the most sobering passages in all the Old Testament. Here God is speaking against the false shepherds and shows his deep love and care for His sheep.

The word of the LORD came to me: [2] "Son of man, prophesy against the shepherds of Israel; prophesy, and say to them, even to the shepherds, Thus says the Lord GOD: Ah, shepherds of Israel who have been feeding yourselves! Should not shepherds feed the sheep? [3] You eat the fat, you clothe yourselves with the wool, you slaughter the fat ones, but you do not feed the sheep. ⁴ The weak you have not strengthened, the sick you have not healed, the injured you have not bound up, the strayed you have not brought back, the lost you have not sought, and with force and harshness you have ruled them. ⁵ So they were scattered, because there was no shepherd, and they became food for all the wild beasts. My sheep were scattered; ⁶ they wandered over all the mountains and on every high hill. My sheep were scattered over all the face of the earth, with none to search or seek for them.

⁷ *"Therefore, you shepherds, hear the word of the LORD: ⁸ As I live, declares the Lord GOD, surely because my sheep have become a prey, and my sheep have become food for all the wild beasts, since there was no shepherd, and because my shepherds have not searched for my sheep, but the shepherds have fed themselves, and have not fed my sheep, ⁹ therefore, you shepherds, hear the word of the LORD: ¹⁰ Thus says the Lord GOD, Behold, I am against the shepherds, and I will require my sheep at their hand and put a stop to their feeding the sheep. No longer shall the shepherds feed themselves. I will rescue my sheep from their mouths, that they may not be food for them.*

¹¹ *"For thus says the Lord GOD: Behold, I, I myself will search for my sheep and will seek them out. ¹² As a shepherd seeks out his flock when he is among his sheep that have been scattered, so will I seek out my sheep, and I will rescue them from all places where they have been scattered on a day of clouds and thick darkness. ¹³ And I will bring them out from the peoples and gather them from the countries, and will bring them into their own land. And I will feed them on the mountains of Israel, by the ravines, and in all the inhabited places of the country. ¹⁴ I will feed*

them with good pasture, and on the mountain heights of Israel shall be their grazing land. There they shall lie down in good grazing land, and on rich pasture they shall feed on the mountains of Israel. ¹⁵ I myself will be the shepherd of my sheep, and I myself will make them lie down, declares the Lord GOD. ¹⁶ I will seek the lost, and I will bring back the strayed, and I will bind up the injured, and I will strengthen the weak, and the fat and the strong I will destroy. I will feed them in justice.

¹⁷ "As for you, my flock, thus says the Lord GOD: Behold, I judge between sheep and sheep, between rams and male goats. ¹⁸ Is it not enough for you to feed on the good pasture, that you must tread down with your feet the rest of your pasture; and to drink of clear water, that you must muddy the rest of the water with your feet? ¹⁹ And must my sheep eat what you have trodden with your feet, and drink what you have muddied with your feet?

²⁰ "Therefore, thus says the Lord GOD to them: Behold, I, I myself will judge between the fat sheep and the lean sheep. ²¹ Because you push with side and shoulder, and thrust at all the weak with your horns, till you have scattered them abroad, ²² I will rescue my flock; they shall no longer be a prey. And I will judge between sheep and sheep. ²⁰ And I will set up over them one shepherd, my servant David, and he shall feed them: he shall feed them and be their shepherd. ²⁴ And I, the LORD, will be their God, and my servant David shall be prince among them. I am the LORD; I have spoken."

The Lord is upset with these false shepherds who don't care for His people and don't feed them. How would shepherds feed sheep, using this comparison? How do shepherds feed sheep? With knowledge and with understanding. Remember the Jeremiah passage we read a moment ago:

"I will give you shepherds after my own heart who will feed you with knowledge and understanding, teaching the word of God faithfully, caring for people genuinely, doing the works that shepherds are called to do."

The under-shepherds, those who have been called by God to shepherd people, have no power in themselves to nourish, or encourage, or strengthen, or comfort, the Lord's people. This is only accomplished when the Lord makes our efforts fruitful.

When the Lord is your Shepherd, you are preserved.

We have seen that when the Lord is your Shepherd, your needs are met. You are cared for, physically, emotionally, and spiritually. You are fed and you are watered. But there's a third thing that is true when the Lord is your Shepherd: **you are preserved, protected.**

Verse 3: *He restores my soul. He leads me in paths of righteousness for his name's sake.*

To restore carries the idea of turning back, to return. He turns back my soul, returns my soul. It can mean that God revives in the sense of giving life again, in the sense of the experience of life, to revive, to refresh. But I think it is more than just refreshment. The idea is that our God doesn't allow us to wander away from Him and to stay lost, as a sheep might wander away from a shepherd. He goes to find the lost and brings it back. In this same way, God deals with us.

This same verb that's translated *restores* here is used in Isaiah 49:5, speaking of Israel, where it says: *And now the LORD says, he who formed me—Israel—from the womb to* *be his servant, to <u>bring</u> Jacob <u>back</u> to him; and that Israel might be gathered to him—for I am honored in the eyes of the Lord, and my God has become my strength...."*

The word is also used in other Psalms:

Psalm 60:1 *O God, you have rejected us, broken our defenses; you have been angry; oh, <u>restore</u> us.*

Psalm 19:7 *The law of the LORD is perfect, <u>reviving</u> the soul; the testimony of the Lord is sure, making wise the simple....*

Now, back to Psalm 23, *He restores my soul.* ***He leads me in the paths of righteousness***. Gerald Wilson, commenting on this says, "The ambiguity of the language and the context allows a moral quality to creep in. If the shepherd and sheep are images of a life fully dependent and trusting on Yahweh, then paths of righteousness take on the meaning of a way of life that fulfills God's expectation for His followers. The sheep are not left to their own devices, but are led by God Himself to take the correct path, the one that gets the sheep where they need to go."[11]

So, how does the Lord ***restore*** the soul? How does the Lord restore me, the self? How does He turn me back? ***He leads me in paths of righteousness***, and that means paths that are more than just straight and right. It means paths that please Him, the path in which I need to travel, the path in which I need to go. In meeting our needs and caring for us, God is at work in the lives of His people to preserve them. So, when we wander outside of the way, He brings us back,

---

[11] Gerald H. Wilson, *Psalms Volume 1* in NIV Application Commentary series (Grand Rapids: Zondervan, 2002), p 433.

setting our feet on paths of righteousness. He doesn't let us go our own way.

Does this mean that His people never fail? Does this mean that His people never are guilty of a bad testimony? Of course not, but what it does mean, is that even <u>after</u> they fail, <u>He doesn't leave them in their failure. He brings us to repentance.</u>

*He leads me in paths of righteousness **for His name's sake**.*

Our ways will either vindicate or bring shame to our Shepherd. Our lives will either tell the truth about His great name and His reputation, or will give a false impression of who the true God really is. And He is the kind of Shepherd who so loves us, and works on behalf of His own name, that with His Word He turns us back and sets our feet on the right pathway.

In the book of Ezekiel, the Lord is about to tell us about the new covenant, and He's going to do something with respect to His people, and says He's doing this not for their sake, **but for the sake of His holy name.**

Ezekiel 36:22 *Therefore say to the house of Israel, Thus says the Lord GOD: It is not for your sake, O house of Israel, that I am about to act, but for the sake of my holy name, which you have profaned among the nations to which you came. [23] And I will vindicate the holiness of my great name, which has been profaned among the nations, and which you have profaned among them. And the nations will know that I am the LORD, declares the Lord GOD, when through you I vindicate my holiness before their eyes. [24] I will take you from the nations and gather you from all the countries and bring you into your own* *land. [25] I will sprinkle clean water on you, and you shall be clean from all your uncleannesses, and from all your idols I will cleanse you. [26] And I will give you a new heart, and a new spirit I will put within you. And I will remove the heart of stone from your flesh and give you a heart of flesh. [27] And I will put my Spirit within you, and cause you to walk in my statutes and be careful to obey my rules. [28] You shall dwell in the land that I gave to your fathers, and you shall be my people, and I will be your God. [29] And I will deliver you from all your uncleannesses. And I will summon the grain and make it abundant and lay no famine upon you. [30] I will make the fruit of the tree and the increase of the field abundant, that you may never again suffer the disgrace of famine among the nations. [31] Then you will remember your evil ways, and your deeds that were not good, and you will loathe yourselves for your iniquities and your abominations. [32] It is not for your sake that I will act, declares the Lord GOD; let that be known to you. Be ashamed and confounded for your ways, O house of Israel.*

Oh, there's a great day of salvation, an outpouring of salvation that is coming. And when God acts, He's going to do it not for their sake, but for His sake, for the sake of His great name. So, what kind of a Shepherd is the Lord? He's the Shepherd who blesses us with great riches. We **lack nothing**, we have everything we need. **He cares for us** in the provision of food, drink, and a place for comfort and rest. He **restores** the soul, turns the soul back, and **leads us in paths of righteousness**. And why does He do it? **For His name's sake, for the sake of His name.**

Here's a wonderful thought: the Lord uses human instruments in the shepherding work that He carries out. **He shepherds His sheep, but He uses under-shepherds**. No matter how faithful we are, we are absolutely helpless to accomplish what is described here. Those of us who are under-shepherds are called to feed the sheep, but in the final analysis, we can teach the Word of God faithfully, but only God Himself, only God's Spirit can take this word and make it sweet to your heart. We will give an account for how faithfully we've carried out our shepherding responsibility, but don't make the mistake of thinking under-shepherds have the ability that only the chief Shepherd has. We can admonish and teach and correct and exhort and plead, but if the Lord doesn't set your feet on paths that lead to righteousness, we are helpless to change you. Even when He's using human instruments, the Lord <u>must</u> be the One who shepherds His sheep, who feeds them with green grass beside still waters.

When you read the Bible on your own, only God can make it pointed and drive it home to your heart. He's the One who restores, turning the heart. So, when your soul is fed and refreshed by the clean water of His Word, thank Him. When your heart is blessed by a sermon or a Bible class lesson or by personal study of the Word, thank Him. When the Lord brings conviction and turns your feet away from paths of sin, look up and thank Him. The only explanation is His shepherding work in your heart.

What should our response be to these wonderful truths? One, we ought to <u>always respond with examination</u>. Do I know what David's describing? Have I known experientially what he describes? *The LORD makes me lie down in green pastures; He leads me beside still waters; He restores my soul; He leads me in paths of righteousness for the sake of His name.* He doesn't leave me to myself; He doesn't let me wander away. Is this really you? Is the Lord your Shepherd?

And then, if you can honestly say, "Yes, the Lord is my Shepherd," the second response is one of celebration. If the Lord is your Shepherd, I ask you, what kind of thanksgiving should be pouring out of your life? What kind of worship should characterize your existence? What kind of testimony should be pouring forth from your lips? How should you be telling the world about your Shepherd, if indeed He is your Shepherd? Is your life one living, breathing, walking, talking, thinking act of celebration to God for the fact that He shepherds you? Then shake off every bit of apathy that has crept into your life, recognizing it for the sorry sin that it is. Shake off apathy and pursue your God for all that He's worth—He's worth everything.

God-Given Assurance

At its heart, the 23rd Psalm is one of confidence in God. It is a confession and a celebration of God's faithfulness, love, and power toward His servant David and toward all His children. David begins with a statement of personal relationship when he says, *The LORD is my shepherd.* Then he lists the riches that belong to this relationship.

From the beginning of the psalm until now, David has spoken of God in the third person, focusing on what He has done: *He makes me lie down in green pastures. He leads me beside still waters. He restores my soul. He leads me in paths of righteousness for his name's sake.* But here in verse 4, notice the language changes. David speaks directly to God, making these statements more personal: *Even though I walk through the valley of the shadow of death, I will fear no evil, for you are with me…*—not "He is with me"…*your rod and your staff, they comfort me. You prepare a table before me in the presence of my enemies; you anoint my head with oil; my cup overflows.* This language reflects his personal relationship with the Lord, not just a theoretical observation. It's not, "Here is what I know is true of God, and therefore, I can draw the conclusion it is true of me." There's nothing wrong or invalid about that, but he's doing something more.

David is now speaking directly to God. "Lord, this is how You have dealt with me personally and experientially." A great test for us, as we look at the remainder of this psalm, is to ask ourselves whether these affirmations can be found in our own hearts. Are these just theoretical statements that we can agree with, or do these statements represent our own assurance in the Lord? Can you say, "Lord, **You** have done this for me; *I will fear no evil, for **You** are with me*"? *"**Your*** *rod and **Your** staff, they comfort me. **You** prepare a table before me in the presence of my enemies."* Are these statements that you can make about your own relationship with God?

A Celebration of Assurance

So, we move from a statement about personal relationship and a survey of riches to **a celebration of assurance**. This is about supernatural assurance, the gift of assurance that God gives to His people. Because verses 1 to 3 are true, we ought to feel the way David does in verses 4 to 6. Everything we've seen thus far in verses 1 to 3 warrants this assurance. In fact, these truths not only warrant it, they require it. We <u>should</u> feel what David feels. God gives us this assurance, yet it is not automatic assurance. Some real Christians still lack it. There are different kinds of assurance…the assurance that <u>God saved us</u>—"I know that I really am one of His sheep, a child of God." There's the assurance for the end of the road, that <u>God will bring us ultimate salvation</u>—"I know that when I die, I'll go to heaven and be in the presence of the Lord." But there's also the assurance that we should feel between those two realities—the assurance that <u>He is our Shepherd today.</u> If the Lord has saved you, and if he will finish your salvation, why should you be anxious, fearing that He won't shepherd you today? If you don't feel that assurance of God's work in your life right now, the way to experience this assurance from the Holy Spirit is through <u>knowing and believing</u> these truths, and then <u>choosing</u> to relate to the Lord based on that knowledge. We need to bring into our everyday experience the knowledge that the Lord has saved us and that He holds onto us, and that we're secure until the end—so He's our Shepherd today.

And so, as believers, we have the opportunity for the Holy Spirit to impart into our hearts the sense of assurance based upon the truth of our relationship to God.

The life of assurance is a life of trust.

Look at verse 4: *Even though I walk through the valley of the shadow of death, I will fear no evil....*

What is this life of assurance? First of all, it's a life of trust. The life of assurance we should have in the present, is that we really trust the Lord. We trust God. <u>You will not know assurance until you know that your life is in God's hand, and there your life is safe</u>. So, even if you *walk through the valley of the shadow of death*, there is no reason to be afraid. Do you know that? Do you believe that?

The phrase, *the shadow of death*, can be understood in a couple of ways. It translates a single Hebrew word, (צַלְמָ֫וֶת ṣal·mā·weṯ) that is made up of two words, one meaning death, the other shadow or darkness. Sometimes, Hebrew compound words express a superlative. So, some have taken this to mean the deepest darkness: *Though I walk through the valley of the deepest darkness*. This particular word is used in the Book of Job several times to speak of just darkness, a place of darkness. But in the Book of Job it is also used to speak clearly, in one place, of the darkness of death. Using the analogy of a shepherd and sheep here, certainly the picture is one of a shepherd leading the sheep through places that could cause great fear. Imagine a shepherd leading the sheep through narrow passageways with steep walls that shut out the light, with dangerous positions on either side of firm footing, and you will get the picture.

Application—

To death

How, then, should we apply this verse? One way it's been applied by the Holy Spirit in the lives of God's people throughout the ages is when they are literally walking through the valley of death, when they are coming to the end of their lives. It is no accident that God's Spirit has comforted many believing hearts with the statement in verse 4 when they were dying.

And when this passage is applied to the death of the saints, it's completely accurate. Our Lord and Savior walked a dark pathway before us, in our place. He was forsaken and bore the wrath of God upon Himself. Because He conquered the grave and the serpent, death no longer holds the believer in bondage. It has no grip on us. As a result, there will be no sting in it for us. So, when a believer makes his way from this life into the presence of our God, know that:

- It is a walk—not a station. We're not stationed in a place of darkness and death. It's just a place we walk through.
- It's a valley—not a prison.
- It is a shadow—Christ endured the substance of death, the reality of it.
- It is darkness—but there is light on the other side. It is both sobering and real, but on the other side is light, as the believer passes into the presence of God. Even where there is darkness, there is no reason for us to fear, because for God, the darkness is as light. There is no difference to Him.

Psalm 139:8 *If I ascend to heaven, you are there!*
If I make my bed in Sheol, you are there!
⁹ If I take the wings of the morning
and dwell in the uttermost parts of the sea,
¹⁰ even there your hand shall lead me,
and your right hand shall hold me.
¹¹ If I say, "Surely the darkness shall cover me,
and the light about me be night,"
¹² even the darkness is not dark to you;
the night is bright as the day,
for darkness is as light with you.

As fellow believers, we can walk through a great many things together, although if the Lord tarries, and we come to the day of our death, we can't walk through that together with one another. But we don't walk that pathway alone, do we? *Yea, though I walk through the valley of the shadow of death, I will fear no evil, for You are with me....*

Application—

To every dark moment of life

The valley of the shadow of death can be applied to the <u>death of the saints</u>, but also to <u>the way we live our lives</u>. That includes every dark moment, even the deepest, darkest times in your life. You can apply it to the darkest times that you walk through <u>regarding relationships</u>. Many of you who read this are hurting in some area of relationship in your life. Maybe it's with your children, or with your husband or wife, or with someone who is persecuting you—dark times relationally.

<u>Sometimes, you walk through valleys emotionally</u>. Discouragement and depression are not strangers to the saints of God. The idea that because you're a Christian, you

will never know depression, is just a false idea. It's false from both from the standpoint of what is revealed in Scripture, and also from what we see in church history. Believers can struggle greatly in the realm of their emotions, and there will be days when we walk through dark times.

Another area where we can experience darkness is in our circumstances, when it seems like there is no way out, and we don't know what the solutions are. Derek Kidner wrote, "The dark valley, or ravine, is as truly one of His 'right paths' as are the green pastures—a fact that takes much of the sting out of any ordeal."[12] We forget that sometimes. We have no problem seeing the green pastures as the pathway that God has destined for us to walk in, but somehow while walking through the valley of the shadow of death, we wonder if we're in the right place. However, the Lord's hand leads us into these places also.

F. B. Meyer wrote a great classic devotional commentary on this Psalm. He said:

> There is a good purpose in all these shadowed valleys.
> They test the quality of the soul. They reveal our weak
> places. They unveil the stars that peer down through
> the interspaces of rock and tree. They make us follow
> the Shepherd closely, lest we lose Him. They teach us
> to value, as never before, the rod and staff. Blessed
> are those who do not see, but who yet believe; and
> who are content to be stripped of all joy and comfort
> and ecstasy, if it be the Shepherd's will, so long as

---

[12]Derek Kidner, *Psalms 1-72* (Downers Grove: InterVarsity Press, 1973), p. 110.

there is left to them the sound of His voice, and the knowledge that He is near.[13]

We all know it. Every believer could stand and testify that some of the closest times of fellowship that you have ever known with our God have been times that were dark times for you. Oh, the Lord does things in these dark valleys in our lives that don't get accomplished in any other way or in any other place.

Affirmation

So, what is David's affirmation concerning these valleys? Verse 4: *Even though I walk through the valley of the shadow of death,* ***I will fear no evil.*** Here's his affirmation: "I will not be afraid. I will not be afraid of harm. I will not be afraid of that which would threaten to destroy me."

Be it in the relational realm, the emotional realm or in the realm of circumstances, I will not be afraid. He is saying that in the darkest of ravines, he trusts that the Shepherd will lead him safely. He trusts that the Shepherd is his security.

Abiding Presence

He gives us the basis for his affirmation in the next statement: *Even though I walk through the valley of the shadow of death, I will fear no evil,*—why not, David?—***for you are with me*** ....

It is God's presence that is his confidence. And the greatest example of what it means to trust God as you walk through a dark valley, knowing that His presence is enough, is our Shepherd, our Savior, the Lord Jesus. He faced such

---

[13] F.B. Meyer, *The Shepherd Psalm*, various editions.

a valley of the shadow of death so that He could even say, *My Father, if it be possible, let this cup pass from me; nevertheless, not as I will, but as you will.* He trusted the Father every step of the way, all the way to the cross. Look at His words the night before his crucifixion.

John 16:32 *Behold, the hour is coming, indeed it has come, when you will be scattered, each to his own home, and will leave me alone. Yet I am not alone, for the Father is with me.*

Indeed, they did scatter. Indeed, the Lord Jesus was all alone. But He wasn't alone, and He knew He wasn't alone, because He rested in the Father's presence. *Even though I walk through the valley of the shadow of death, I will fear no evil, for you are with me....*

Consider Psalm 91. It is no coincidence that we have a verse that refers to the Messiah in the midst of this psalm.

¹ He who dwells in the shelter of the Most High
*   will abide in the shadow of the Almighty.*
² I will say to the Lord, "My refuge and my fortress,
*   my God, in whom I trust."*

³ For he will deliver you from the snare of the fowler
*   and from the deadly pestilence.*
⁴ He will cover you with his pinions,
*   and under his wings you will find refuge;*
*   his faithfulness is a shield and buckler.*
⁵ You will not fear the terror of the night,
*   nor the arrow that flies by day,*
⁶ nor the pestilence that stalks in darkness,
*   nor the destruction that wastes at noonday.*

[7] A thousand may fall at your side,
ten thousand at your right hand,
but it will not come near you.
[8] You will only look with your eyes
and see the recompense of the wicked.
[9] Because you have made the Lord your dwelling
place—
the Most High, who is my refuge—
[10] no evil shall be allowed to befall you,
no plague come near your tent.

[11] For he will command his angels concerning you
to guard you in all your ways.
[12] On their hands they will bear you up,
lest you strike your foot against a stone.
[13] You will tread on the lion and the adder;
the young lion and the serpent you will trample
underfoot.

[14] "Because he holds fast to me in love, I will
deliver him;
I will protect him, because he knows my name.

[15] When he calls to me, I will answer him;
I will be with him in trouble;
I will rescue him and honor him.
With long life I will satisfy him
and show him my salvation."

Friend, the Scripture says that everyone who knows the name of God (those who truly know His character) puts their trust in Him.[14] To know His name is to know that He is trustworthy.

---

[14] Psalm 9:10.

The life of assurance is a life of security.

Look back at Psalm 23. So, David expresses his confidence in the Lord. This is the life of assurance, the assurance that you have when the Lord is your Shepherd. You can trust Him even in the darkest place, even in the deepest valley. But now there's a second expression of assurance. The life of assurance is not only a life of trust, it is **a life of security**.

Verse 4b: *your rod and your staff, they comfort me.*

We are secure and comforted because we are safe, protected, guarded and guided. The *rod* is for protection. It has a short handle, larger at the top, used for fighting off predators and for defending against robbers. The *staff* is more like a walking stick. You've seen pictures of the shepherd's crook, used to guide the sheep, to keep them in order, to rescue them when they're in places that are hard to reach. Both the rod and the staff can be symbols of discipline. Most of the time when the word for *rod* clearly refers to a rod (it is often used to refer to a scepter), it is used in a context of discipline.

So, David, thinking about God as his Shepherd, takes comfort in the knowledge of his rod and his staff. The Psalmist has an attentive Shepherd who is always on duty, never absent, never distracted. The sheep are not left to their own desires. Their fate is not determined by their own choices. The Shepherd watches over the sheep—redirecting them, guiding them, rescuing them.

- He knows His sheep.
- His sheep know Him.

- He will not lose a single one of them.
- His sheep are safe in His hand. No one will snatch them away.

This is what Jesus said:

John 10:27 *My sheep hear my voice, and I know them, and they follow me. [28] I give them eternal life, and they will never perish, and no one will snatch them out of my hand. [29] My Father, who has given them to me, is greater than all, and no one is able to snatch them out of the Father's hand. [30] I and the Father are one.*

This is security! You can trust Him. Even in the darkest valley, you can trust Him. His rod and His staff should comfort you. His eye is upon you. You're not lost to Him. You are safe in His hand, and He will not let you go, and no one will ever snatch you away.

Now, we would love to be able to say that most of the time when the Shepherd is rescuing and redirecting us, it's because of something an enemy has done to us. We'd love to be able to say, "I'm in that ditch because of my enemies, and the Lord is constantly rescuing me from my enemies."

Unfortunately, I think every true child of God knows better than that. Most of the rescuing work and most of the redirecting work that God has done in our lives, has not been because of an enemy. It's been because of our own foolishness and disobedience. It has been because of our own waywardness. When the Shepherd is rescuing sheep, it is usually because His sheep have gotten themselves into trouble. Isn't that right? Meyer captured this very well:

> …very often sin not only grieves Him, but it plunges us into circumstances of misery and trouble which threaten to

overwhelm us. At such times He is not unmindful of His own; and though we may seem to have forfeited all claim to His care, yet He is 'a very present help in time of trouble;' He does not permit us to reap what we have sown. He averts the full penalty of our own mistakes and misdeeds. He comes after us in the wilderness, not staying his foot until He has discovered the pit into which we have fallen, from which He does not fail to drag us forth; placing us on His shoulders if we are too weak to walk, and bringing us back; satisfied with no other recompense than that we are safe....Oh the long-suffering patience of Christ, who will not permit us to be overwhelmed by the sorrows and penalties which we may have incurred, but will reach out His crook to drag us back from the death that we had courted![15]

What a fabulous description that is, and what an accurate one. If the Lord had allowed us to go our own way, where would we be? How often have we courted death in terms of our own choices, only for God to extend His staff and with that crook pull us out of the ditch that we're in and set our feet on straight paths— to the glory of His name!

When you realize that, you begin to see what really makes sin sinful. I pray that the Lord would teach us that the greatest way of seeing the sinfulness of our sin is not by measuring our sins <u>against the law of God,</u> but by measuring our sins <u>against the love of God.</u> The law of God identifies our sins, but the love of God magnifies our sins, because the Lord has been good to us despite our sinfulness. The Lord has loved us despite our waywardness. When we willfully choose to go against the will of our God, we are not just sinning against His law, but against all of the overwhelming

---

[15] Ibid. p.88-89

expressions of His love toward us, which is constant, faithful, trustworthy and true.

Do you see that? Is your heart broken over your sinfulness and your disobedience? And is what breaks your heart not just the knowledge that it is against the law of God, but also that it is in the face of the love of God? And yet, how faithful our Shepherd is, not to deal with us according to our sins, but according to His mercy.

Psalm 130:3 *If you, O LORD, should mark iniquities, O Lord, who could stand?*

So, the Lord is our Shepherd if we're His people, your Shepherd if you belong to Him. What does that mean? It means that **He is worthy of your trust.** Even when you're walking through the valley of the shadow of death, there is no reason to fear, because He's with you. So, if He's worthy of your trust, if you really are safe, then trust Him.

Do you need to trust Him? Maybe you feel like you're in a dark, dark place, and you're afraid. If the Lord is your Shepherd, though you walk through the valley of the shadow of death, do not fear. He is there. When the Lord is your Shepherd, He is in charge of your safety, and you are secure. There is His rod that will fight off the predators, and there is His staff that will keep you in line, and even pull you out of the mud. The Lord is your Shepherd. **He is your safety.** Now, will you rest in that knowledge? Will you recognize that your whole life is really in His charge, that He really is in control?

My friend, whenever you think you're in control, it is just a mirage, an imagination. Your life is in His hand. Will you rest there? And then, when you recognize this, will you love Him for it? Will you discover that your greatest motivation to live a life that honors His name, is that you are loved by Him, and you, therefore, love Him back?

The Lord Is My Host

In the last chapter, we discussed that a believer's life is one of assurance—affirming that we can trust the Lord as our Shepherd, and we are safe and protected with Him. Now in verse 5, this celebration of assurance continues, but the language changes because the comparison changes. In the first 4 verses, the Lord is pictured as a Shepherd, but **in verse 5 He is pictured as a host.** There's a lesson even in this. The life of security that we enjoy with our God is so great that one comparison is not sufficient for David. The Shepherd analogy is helpful to us, but now the picture is of God's people, in this case represented by David himself, as he's in the presence of God, in the house of God, and being hosted by God.

You prepare a table before me in the presence of my enemies; you anoint my head with oil; my cup overflows. Surely goodness and mercy shall follow me all the days of my life, and I shall dwell in the house of the LORD forever.

It's true that most of the time in the Psalms, when it mentions the house of the Lord, it's referring to the tabernacle or the temple, but I think in this case, it ought to be taken as a metaphor. You are in the house of God, in a royal palace, and He is your host. Verses 5 and 6 give us an even greater and clearer picture of what it means to live out this life of assurance when you really belong to God.

The believer's assurance is a life of refuge.

We've seen that this life of assurance is one of trust and security, **but in verse 5 we see that it is also a life of refuge,** *You prepare a table before me in the presence of my enemies....*

In Old Testament times, when a host received you and you shared their table, enmities were put away. The host assumed the responsibility for your care and safety. Only an untrustworthy host would have you sit at his table and then betray you or harm you or expose you to danger while you were under his care. This was carried to such an extreme that in Genesis 19, Lot's guests had to prevent him from sacrificing his daughters' safety for their own. You see the very same commitment on the part of a host in Judges 19.[16]

Proverbs 23 describes a worthless man whom you ought to beware of if you sit at his table.

Proverbs 23:6 *Do not eat the bread of a man who is stingy; do not desire his delicacies, for he is like one who is inwardly calculating.* [7] *"Eat and drink!" he says to you, but his heart is not with you.* [8] *You will vomit up the morsels that you have eaten, and waste your pleasant words.*

When it says that this kind of host is stingy, it literally means he has an evil eye. This is a worthless man. He can't be trusted, and he's not honest. But God is not that kind of host. When He sets a table for you, it's because He genuinely cares for you and has taken responsibility for you. You are safe in His presence.

God is not a worthless host. He receives the believer to Himself, and therefore assumes the responsibility for his care. God is a trustworthy provider and protector for him.

In these verses God has prepared a table for David in the presence of his enemies. We still have enemies. They

---

[16] Here a Levite goes to retrieve his concubine from her father's house, and the father insists on him staying for several days.

haven't gone away, but we are safe and provided for in the house of God, having come under the shelter of His care. Even though our enemies may be right there, still full of malice and hatred, we are safe because God has assumed the responsibility for our safety. This is the kind of host He is.

I wonder how often it is that as believers, though we are safe, we don't feel safe, but are afraid, as if God has not taken responsibility for our care. We're told we're safe in His hand, and that no one can snatch us out, yet we still live fearfully. We act as if He's received us to Himself, but now can't be trusted to protect us. Be assured, you are no safer in this world than when you are in the house of God, in the accepting presence of God.

Before continuing, do you feel that safety, even though you're aware of enemies and at times may be tempted to be afraid of that which threatens you? Even then, do you recognize that you are safe because, through faith in Christ, you now have a saving relationship with God and live your life in His accepting presence? If you are a child of God, then you are within the shelter of His house.

The believer's assurance is a life of fellowship.

FELLOWSHIP IN SALVATION

Next, notice that the believer's life of assurance **is a life of communion, or we could say, a life of fellowship.** The picture is, God has set a table for us. To be at the Lord's table is to enjoy His fellowship, to share in communion. And we need to be clear about that.

As we share the gospel, serving as ambassadors for Christ and as evangelists to the world, we need to be clear with this world about what salvation is. Sometimes, and rightly so, we focus on the legal aspects of salvation: redemption, justification, reconciliation and forgiveness. But we often neglect to talk about the experiential side of salvation, where you go from being someone who was estranged from God, to being someone who has fellowship with God.

According to John 17:3, having eternal life means you know the Father and you know His Son. That is eternal life, to know the Father and to know His Son. And when the Apostle John declares the gospel in 1 John chapter 1, what is he inviting people into? **Fellowship** with the Father and with His Son and with God's people.

So, being saved means you now have fellowship with God. You have a relationship with Him that is personal and real. It's not empty, formal, dead religion. It's not just attendance in a building, or going through religious activity. It is a real relationship with God that has been established, based upon the finished work of His Son Jesus Christ. It is to be brought into the very presence of God, and the mediator of that relationship is His Son.

The New Testament mentions many different kinds of fellowship that exist in this salvation relationship:

- fellowship with the Father

- fellowship with His Son

- the fellowship of the Holy Spirit

- the fellowship of the gospel

- the fellowship of the sufferings of Christ

- the fellowship of the saints

- the fellowship of sharing materially, both with our finances and meeting needs

All sorts of fellowship exists in this relationship of salvation.

1 Corinthians 1:9 *God is faithful, by whom you were called into the fellowship of his Son, Jesus Christ our Lord.*

2 Corinthians 13:14 *The grace of the Lord Jesus Christ and the love of God and the fellowship of the Holy Spirit be with you all.*

1 John 1:3 *That which we have seen and heard we proclaim also to you, so that you too may have fellowship with us; and indeed our fellowship is with the Father and with his Son Jesus Christ.*

This is what salvation is—fellowship with God. (If you're not in the fellowship, you're not saved.) What has God done for His people? He has set a table, and now you sit in His presence, enjoying **fellowship** with Him. And you are safe there, even in the presence of your enemies.

HOW TO ENJOY THIS FELLOWSHIP

As a side note, how do you enjoy that fellowship? Salvation is to be in the fellowship, but the truth is, we're not always enjoying that fellowship the way that we can as believers. Maybe you're going through a dry time right now, and your fellowship with God doesn't seem as rich as it did in the past. How do you practically enjoy the fellowship that you entered into through faith in Christ? Here are a couple of reminders.

One, <u>you have to be aware of the reality of it</u>. You need to practice the knowledge of this fellowship every day, throughout the day. I could make it as simple as this: Have you been mindful of God today? Has this relationship been on your mind? Did you get up this morning and begin to go through your day as though you don't have fellowship with God at all? Wouldn't that be a sad thing, to be someone who has entered into fellowship with God, and yet to live your life as though the fellowship doesn't exist? So, one, you're mindful of it.

Two, then <u>you have to engage in that fellowship throughout the day.</u> God has invited us—in fact, He has commanded us—to approach Him in prayer, in worship.

Hebrews 4:16 *Let us then with confidence draw near to the throne of grace, that we may receive mercy and find grace to help in time of need.*

Have you done that today? Have you drawn near to the throne of God's grace? Have you actively sought His face this day? Have you communed with the Lord through prayer and Bible study and worshipful serving activity? Today when you went to work, did you work as unto the Lord? Today, as you've related with your family, have you done that mindful of the fact that even this is worship?

HOW TO IMPROVE YOUR ENJOYMENT OF

FELLOWSHIP WITH THE LORD

Besides being mindful of it and engaged, there is something else to do if we want to enjoy this fellowship. We can improve our enjoyment of it by <u>pursuing righteousness</u> on the one hand and <u>putting away sin</u> on the other hand. What is it that gets in the way of our fellowship with God?

It's sin. What is it that will rob you of the joy of salvation? It's sin. Or, if you want to put it into the language of love, the way you improve your enjoyment of this fellowship is by <u>loving God</u> and <u>loving people</u>. Today, have you lived your life loving God and loving your neighbor?

Do not imagine, or pretend within your mind and heart, that you can love God while mistreating people, or that you can mistreat people and still enjoy your fellowship with God.

1 Peter 3:7 makes this principle clear: *Likewise, husbands, live with your wives in an understanding way, showing honor to the woman as the weaker vessel, since they are heirs with you of the grace of life, so that your prayers may not be hindered.* You cannot mistreat your wife and then go into your prayer closet and think it's going to be effective.

The believer's assurance is a life of divine generosity.

The believer's assurance is also a life of divine generosity. This life of celebrating and enjoying the assurance that we have in a saving relationship with Christ, is one of <u>experiencing, acknowledging and receiving divine generosity.</u> Notice in verse 5, He prepares a table. There's a feast. There's food to enjoy and there's a cup.

You prepare a table before me in the presence of my enemies; you anoint my head with oil; my cup overflows.

This cup is not just full—it's overflowing!

May I remind you that our God is not just a host. He's a liberal host. <u>He delights in blessing His people, and He blesses them lavishly.</u> The book *The New Manners and Customs of the Bible* gives an illustration. "In a book published in the early 1800's, *Oriental Customs*, a Captain Wilson wrote about an experience he had that was like that spoken of by the Psalmist. 'I once had this ceremony performed on me in the house of a great and rich Indian in the presence of a large company. The gentleman of the house poured upon my hands and arms a delightful odoriferous perfume, put a golden cup into my hands, and poured wine into it until it ran over, assuring me at the same time that it was a great pleasure to him to receive me, and that I should find a rich supply of my needs in his house.'"[17]

God doesn't just set a table. He doesn't just fill your cup. It overflows. Do you recognize that the Lord, your Shepherd and host, has blessed you lavishly? He loves you and is no miser.

2 Corinthians 9:6 *The point is this: whoever sows sparingly will also reap sparingly, and whoever sows bountifully will also reap bountifully. [7] Each one must give as he has decided in his heart, not reluctantly or under compulsion, for God loves a cheerful giver [8] And God is able to make all grace abound to you, so that having* **all sufficiency in all things at all times** *you may abound in every good work. [9] As it is written,*

"*He has distributed freely, he has given to the poor;*
his righteousness endures forever."

[10] *He who supplies seed to the sower and bread for food will supply and multiply your seed for sowing and increase the harvest of your righteousness.*

---

[17] Freeman, J. M., & Chadwick, H. J. (1998). *Manners & customs of the Bible* (314). North Brunswick, NJ: Bridge-Logos Publishers.

Why would God love a cheerful giver? Because man is made in the image of God, and our cheerful giving reflects his generosity.

Friend, there's not one thing you've ever sown that didn't come from the hand of God. He gives us everything we need, not just to serve Him, but to serve Him abundantly, to serve Him generously in our service to others.

2 Corinthians 9:11 *You will be enriched in every way to be generous in every way, which through us will produce thanksgiving to God.* *[12] For the ministry of this service is not only supplying the needs of the saints but is also overflowing in many thanksgivings to God.*

The Lord's generosity and lavish supply allow us to serve Him by providing generously for others. Then it all overflows in thanksgiving to God. This is the nature and character of God.

Ephesians 1:3 says this—*Blessed be the God and Father of our Lord Jesus Christ, who has blessed us in Christ with every spiritual blessing in the heavenly places....* We don't have <u>some</u> blessing in Jesus. We have <u>all</u> blessing in Jesus. He has blessed us with <u>every</u> spiritual blessing in the heavenly places.

Romans 8:16-17 says, *The Spirit himself bears witness with our spirit that we are children of God, and if children, then heirs—heirs of God and fellow heirs with Christ....*

What has the Lord done for you? If you're a child of God, He has made you one of His heirs. In fact, you are a fellow-heir with His Son. **This is the life of assurance; a life of experiencing divine generosity, the Lord supplying for us in a lavish, unimaginable way.**

The believer's assurance is a life of divine graciousness (kindness).

We find another aspect of this life of assurance in verse 5. It's a life of not only divine generosity**, but a life of divine graciousness, or we could say divine kindness.** He says, *You anoint my head with oil....*

'Again, this is the picture of a host having someone in his home. There's a table, a cup that overflows, and **there's an anointing**. We tend to think about an anointing in association with setting apart kings or prophets, or we think about the application of oil as a medicine, and in that sense, people are anointed in a medicinal way.

But in biblical times, people were also anointed as an act of refreshment. These oils were mixed with fragrances, and people were anointed when they entered a home. It was not uncommon for the host to provide this anointing of the head so that their guests were refreshed. Or, someone might apply oil to themselves in this refreshing manner.

Ruth 3:1 *Then Naomi her mother-in-law said to her, "My daughter, should I not seek rest for you, that it may be well with you? ² Is not Boaz our relative, with whose young women you were? See, he is winnowing barley tonight at the threshing floor. ³ Wash therefore and **anoint yourself**, and put on your cloak and go down to the threshing floor, but do not make yourself known to the man until he has finished eating and drinking."*

Matthew 6:17 *But when you fast, **anoint your head** and wash your face,*—an act of refreshment.

In Luke 7, Jesus has entered the home of a Pharisee named Simon, and a woman of the city, in all likelihood a prostitute who has met Christ earlier, who has been forgiven of her sins, weeps at the feet of Jesus. With her tears, begins to wash His feet. She's brought oil in with her. She wants to anoint His head. And Simon says within himself, "If this man were a prophet, He would know what kind of woman is doing this." And Jesus, proving that He's more than a prophet, knows the thoughts of Simon and addresses the thoughts of Simon:

Luke 7:44 *Then turning toward the woman he said to Simon, "Do you see this woman? I entered your house; you gave me no water for my feet, but she has wet my feet with her tears and wiped them with her hair.* ⁴⁵ *You gave me no kiss, but from the time I came in she has not ceased to kiss my feet.* ⁴⁶ ***You did not anoint my head with oil, but she has anointed my feet with ointment.***"

It's as if Jesus is saying, "You are a rude host who has no understanding of who I am. You've not loved Me as she has loved Me." But you see, one of the ways that Simon had proven himself to be thoughtless, is that **he did not anoint** the head of Christ with oil.

So, the picture here in Psalm 23 is that when you enter the Lord's house and sit at His table, He takes care of you. He is gracious, kind, and thoughtful toward you. His presence is refreshing.

If your spiritual life has seemed dry lately, and you need some refreshment, where do you think you're going to find it? You will find it as you pursue and enjoy the fellowship that you have with God. He is gracious and kind. He refreshes us and takes care of us.

The life of assurance is a life of gracious expectation.

As we move to verse 6, we see something else about this life of assurance. **It is a life of gracious expectation.** Because of the grace of God—this is why I say gracious expectation—there are several things you can expect as a child of God, things you can look forward to and can be certain of.

Verse 6: *Surely goodness and mercy shall follow me all the days of my life, and I shall dwell in the house of the LORD forever.*

First of all, believer, what can you expect from the time that you have come into this presence of God, from the time that you have entered into this fellowship with God, and for the rest of your days on this earth?

David says, *Surely goodness shall follow me.* Literally, good things. Just let that sink in. For the rest of the believer's life, you can expect good things. **For the rest of your life**—I want to say it again—for the rest of your life, **your certain expectation is that you will meet with good things.**

Does that sound like an exaggeration, or is that completely in agreement with something you find in the New Testament, which confirms our interpretation of this? Have you been told in the New Testament that you can always expect good things?

Romans 8:28 *And we know that for those who love God all things work together for **good**...*

For the rest of your life you, believer, can expect that everything is working together for good. In David's words, *goodness will follow* you—literally, good things.

That might be doubted if not for the second statement. Not only will goodness follow us, but **there is *mercy*.** It's the Hebrew word חֶסֶד (chesed). It means steadfast lovingkindness, or covenant faithfulness. It's a great word in the Old Testament. The idea is that the mercy of God, the faithfulness of God, or His steadfast love will follow you for the rest of your days, now that you've entered into the His presence. So, you can be assured that God's love will work everything together for good for the rest of your days, even though it doesn't seem that way from our vantage point.

There's another word we can use to describe the relationship of God's goodness and mercy to us: Relentlessness. Notice the words *follow me.*

Surely goodness and mercy shall follow me. The Hebrew word there means to pursue, to chase. The Bible says *the wicked flee when no one pursues.* At times, believers are very aware of being chased by all sorts of enemies. But what we lose sight of is this—constantly, relentlessly, for the rest of our days on this earth, what is really chasing after us, pursuing us, constantly at our heels, is the goodness and faithfulness of God. We can't escape it or run from it. It's always there.

God loves you relentlessly. He is good to you relentlessly. God is faithful to you relentlessly, without fail. That leads to another word we can use, permanence. How long will this go on? All the days of your life.

Is that not the grace of God? That He would bring you into a relationship with Himself, one that you did not seek on your own, one that you certainly do not deserve, and would have never chosen if He had not changed your desires. God has had grace upon your soul and has brought you into a saving knowledge of His Son. Having redeemed you and brought you to Himself, now He commits Himself to you for the rest of your days. All that you'll know are good things, and His faithfulness, even during all the difficulties of this earthly life: when things are tough, when you're persecuted, your health fails, when finances are tough, and even when a loved one precedes you in death. Whatever your situation is, even then, all you'll know, if you could just see it, is the goodness and faithfulness of God. **It is relentless. It is permanent**.

So then, what can you expect for eternity? If this is what God has made Himself responsible for, for the rest of your days, what about beyond these days? *...and I shall dwell in the house of the* LORD *forever.* **Forever**.

The believer's sure expectation is the enjoyment of the presence of God, the graciousness of God, the goodness of God, the kindness of God, the love and care of God, forever and ever and ever and ever. What a Shepherd! What a host!

Thoughts for self-examination

Is this really true of you? Is this really your position? Does this really apply to you? Are you in the fellowship through faith in God's Son, Jesus? Do you know the Father and the Son? Do you have eternal life? Do you have fellowship with God's people? Have you known what it is to go from darkness to light? Spiritual death to life in God's Son? Has your heart been changed from one that is stone in relation to God Himself and everything that has been revealed by Him? Is it now a heart of flesh that receives His commandments and trembles before His Word, and longs to live a life that pleases Him?

It would be tragic for you to take the words of this psalm and apply them to yourself, if they don't really apply to you. You must first be able to say, due to God's grace, in truth, "The Lord is my Shepherd."

If you can't say that, the good news is, He had you read this book. Would recognize your sinful lost condition, and desire to turn to God from your sin, from your own way, to embrace His Son as God's sacrifice for your sins, and the resurrected Lord of your life? If you will receive Christ, right now, you'll discover what the presence of God really is, and join us in this fellowship that is eternal life.

Study Questions

Psalm 4, Peace in Turbulent Times

1. Would you describe your current times as turbulent? Why or why not?
2. If you are in turbulent times, is it affecting your sleep?
3. Have you pondered the fact that you can expect God to be as faithful in the future as He's been in the past?
4. When in deep troubles, some people run to the Lord and some run away from Him. Which is your pattern? What does that say about your faith?
5. Have people ever dishonored and defamed you because of Jesus Christ? If so, would you ever consider urging them to stop it for their own good?
6. Have you seen your own anger as a danger, as a possible gateway to sinning?
7. Have you learned the safety of stopping in the middle of your anger to be silent and to ponder and even to sleep before taking angry actions?
8. What was wrong with Absalom's sacrifices in 2 Samuel 15:12? How can you be sure that you're not like Absalom? And what must change before David's enemies can offer right sacrifices?
9. How should we process our fears?
10. What three truths are in verses 7-9?
11. Where is your hope?
12. Where is your greatest joy?
13. Where is your main source of protection?
14. Would this be a good Psalm for you to memorize?

Psalm 39, The Wise Response to a Troubled Heart

1. When you see a crowd of people, or see groups of cars or houses or apartments with people in them, how often do you think about the spiritual state of those people? What does your answer say about your own spiritual state?
2. Have you been going through difficulties such as suffering, trials, or hard struggles lately?
3. How can reflecting on life's brevity lead to wisdom?
4. Why do we sometimes need to muzzle our mouths when in the presence of the wicked?
5. When your world seems like it's falling apart, do you usually run <u>to</u> the Lord, or <u>away from</u> the Lord? What will be the usual outcome of these two different courses of action?
6. If we already know that life is brief, why would we ask the Lord to make us know that?
7. What are some ways that people treat temporal (time-bound) things like they are eternal things?
8. Some people view this life as solid, and the life to come as shadowy. Others view this life as a mere shadow, and the life to come as solid reality. Which view is yours? What difference will it make?
9. Right now, today, what are you hoping for? Where was David's hope?
10. David asked to be delivered from his transgressions (his sins). Could your own current struggles be caused, at least in part, by your sins? If so, can you make David's prayer yours?

11. What's the difference between David's attitude in this psalm, and the attitude of a person who rants at God, angry about being in trouble?
12. Will you dare to read this psalm aloud, making David's entire prayer your own?

Psalm 23, The Lord Is My Shepherd

The Lord Is My Shepherd

1. Do you remember when you first read or heard the 23rd Psalm?
2. There are lots of true ways that you can think of God— as Father, as King, as Judge, and so on. Do you often think of Him as Shepherd? If so, what difference does it make? If not, what difference will it make if you think of Him often as your Shepherd?
3. Why is it astounding that the God of the whole universe would want to be your Shepherd?
4. In what way can the statement, "The Lord is my shepherd," search us?
5. What adjectives were used in ALL CAPS to describe our Shepherd?
6. Would you want someone to read (or quote) this psalm to you if you were sitting stunned and exhausted, facing a dangerous and depressing situation? If you were preparing for death?
7. What are some of the qualities of the Lord that are comforting if He is your Shepherd?
8. How can you know whether the Lord is really your Shepherd? If He isn't yet yours, or if you are not sure, what will you do about it?

God-Given Assurance

1. Is the idea that assurance comes from God a new idea to you?

2. This section mentions 3 kinds of assurance: Assurance that God has saved us, assurance that God will bring ultimate salvation, and assurance that He is our Shepherd today. Do you have all three of these? Is one of them harder or easier for you to accept than the others?

3. Have you ever been in a situation where you thought you might die very soon? If so, in that "valley of the shadow of death," were your thoughts of the Lord reassuring or terrifying?

4. If death for the believer is a walk, a valley, a shadow and temporary darkness, instead of a station, a prison, the ultimate substance, and permanent darkness, how does that impact your thoughts concerning death?

5. Are you walking through a dark valley right now? Or is your life sunny? Either way, can seeing dark valleys as part of God's "right paths" for you help you or others through such valleys?

6. Have you ever received a blessing by going through dark valley that you would never have chosen?

7. How can knowledge of the Lord's presence drive out our fears?

8. What's the difference between the shepherd's rod and his staff? How are both of them a comfort to us?

9. Explain the difference between measuring our sins against the law of God and measuring our sins against the love of God.

10. Imagine being a sheep in danger—a danger that may be known or unknown to the sheep. What difference would having a good shepherd make? Now think of your own

situation. What difference does having the Lord as your Shepherd make?

A Survey of Riches

1. What does it mean to you that the Lord is your Shepherd?
2. How are pastors of churches under-shepherds? Is there a danger of thinking of a particular church as "Pastor So-and-So's church?"
3. How can we know that we'll have everything we need? Is there a difference between what you need and what you want?
4. If the Lord promises that we won't lack anything, why do we work?
5. Since the Lord makes his people lie down in green pastures, how does that indicate his active care for us?
6. Why do sheep want green pastures?
7. What lesson does God's generous provision for us tell us concerning how we should meet the needs of others?
8. Is there ever a sense in which the Lord causes you, his sheep, to lie down in the green pastures instead of continuing to work in them? (Take a look at Psalm 127.)
9. Are you more aware of the Lord's provision for your physical needs, or for your spiritual needs? How does He give you food and water to your spirit?
10. In what sense or senses does the Lord preserve you?
11. What's the difference between right paths and righteous paths? Or is there a difference?
12. What does *for your name's sake* mean? What does our path have to do with His name?

13. Is the Lord with you? How do you know?

14. What difference does His presence make when you're in a life-or-death situation? Have you had such an experience?

15. How do you think of death—as a permanent station? As a prison? As nothingness? Or as something to walk through? (What difference does it make that Jesus has died?)

16. Have you ever experienced the Lord's presence, assurance, provision and protection in a special way when you were in a desperate situation? If so, have you thanked Him lately for what He did for you then?

The Lord Is My Host

1. What is the best banquet you've ever attended? What made it outstanding? How did your host make it special?

2. When you're in a tough or scary situation, what difference will it make if you remember that the Lord is your host who has taken your safety upon Himself?

3. If the Lord prepares a table before you in the presence of your enemies, what does that say about his thoughts toward you?

4. "To be at the Lord's table is to enjoy His fellowship, to share in communion." Are you enjoying His fellowship? If so, what are some of the ways or reasons? If not, why not?

5. What does each of the following mean to you? Have you found joy in each?
    a. Fellowship with God the Father
    b. Fellowship with Jesus
    c. The fellowship of the Holy Spirit
    d. The fellowship of the gospel
    e. The fellowship of the sufferings of Christ

     f.   The fellowship with the saints

     g.   The fellowship of sharing materially

6. Before reading this chapter, was "generous" a word you would have used to describe God?

7. Would people describe you as generous?

8. Why would someone anoint a head with oil? Why is it a good thing for the Lord to anoint you?

9. Why can you be confident when facing all of the difficulties of the rest of your life?

10. Are you aware of goodness and mercy following you relentlessly?

11. Do you think of yourself just visiting the Lord's place now and then, or as having a permanent home in the Lord's house forever?